GUIDELINES *for the* LORD'S TABLE MEETING *and the* PURSUIT IN LIFE

Witness Lee

Living Stream Ministry
Anaheim, CA • www.lsm.org

© 2005 Living Stream Ministry

First Edition, February 2005.

ISBN 0-7363-2826-2

Published by

Living Stream Ministry
2431 W. La Palma Ave., Anaheim, CA 92801 U.S.A.
P. O. Box 2121, Anaheim, CA 92814 U.S.A.

Printed in the United States of America

05   06   07   08   09   10   /   9   8   7   6   5   4   3   2   1

CONTENTS

PREFACE

This book is composed of messages given by Brother Witness Lee in 1952 in a training for all the churches in Taiwan. These messages present the proper understanding we should have and pay attention to for the meetings in the church life, particularly the proper preparation and exercise needed for the Lord's table meeting. They also give general guidelines for the pursuit in life. These messages were not reviewed by the speaker.

CHAPTER ONE

CONCERNING BREAKING THE BREAD IN REMEMBRANCE OF THE LORD

Scripture Reading: Matt. 26:26-30; Luke 22:19-20; John 6:53-58

The content of the church is Christ, and the intrinsic reality of every single matter in the church is Christ Himself. If we do not touch Christ and gain Christ, even our worship and service will be meaningless. Just as the reality of believing in the Lord is Christ's coming into us, and the reality of baptism is our union with Christ, so also all the services in the church should be related to Christ.

After a person is saved, he encounters several things. The first is baptism, and the second is the breaking of bread.

BREAD BREAKING

What is the meaning of bread breaking? And what is the reality of bread breaking? Once we mention the breaking of bread, almost all Christians will say that breaking bread is for remembering the Lord. It is true that in the Bible the Lord Himself said that we should break bread in remembrance of Him (Luke 22:19). Thus, based on this word, many Christians conclude that the significance of bread breaking is the remembrance of the Lord. Although this word, this definition, is not wrong, the meaning of remembering the Lord is not simple.

The remembrance spoken of by the Lord is different from our thought concerning remembrance. When we talk about remembrance, we have our own concept. What is this concept? For example, after a father dies, his children remember him. We all understand this kind of remembrance, but is this remembrance the same as our remembrance of the Lord? I am afraid that many people would say that our remembrance of the Lord is simply our meditating on the Lord. This kind of concept, however, is very different from the thought of the Bible.

REMEMBERING THE LORD
NOT BEING MEDITATING ON THE LORD

According to our natural concept, we think that when we break bread in remembrance of the Lord, we must calm down and meditate on the Lord in a detailed way. We feel that we need to contemplate how God came down to the earth from the heavens, was born in a manger, lived in Nazareth for thirty years, trod through Galilee and the land of Judea, suffered man's reproach and persecution, was betrayed, bound, and scourged for us, bore the cross to Golgotha, was crucified, endured unbearable pain, bore our sins, and was judged by God on our behalf. Moreover, we feel that we need to contemplate His burial, His resurrection, His ascension, and His sending of the Holy Spirit. We also feel that we need to contemplate the fact that He is now sitting in the heavens as our High Priest and that one day He will come again to take us to be with Him forever to enjoy His glory in eternity. We have all these scenes within us—from the throne in the heavens to the manger in Bethlehem, from Galilee to Judea, from the virgin Mary to Golgotha, and from the tomb to resurrection, ascension, the second coming, the rapture to be with the Lord, and the enjoyment of glory forever. However, this kind of remembrance is based upon a kind of religious concept that is void of any revelation or spiritual value.

All the terms and all the utterances in the Bible are different from our natural comprehension of things. The faith referred to in the Bible is different from our understanding of faith. The repentance mentioned in the Bible is different from our comprehension of repentance. And the remembrance spoken of in the Bible is definitely not according to our realization of remembrance. When we remember the Lord in the Lord's table meeting every Lord's Day, concentrating in our mind to meditate on the Lord Jesus silently, does this mean that we all love the Lord, are spiritual, and have the Lord's presence? This kind of remembrance by meditation is not the result of revelation but is a kind of religious worship. This is not service that is according to revelation but service that is according to our natural concept.

TO REMEMBER THE LORD
BEING TO EAT THE LORD'S BODY
AND DRINK THE LORD'S BLOOD

In the Bible the Lord does not tell us to meditate on Him in our remembrance of Him. What then did the Lord say? While eating the final Passover, He "took a loaf and gave thanks, and He broke it and gave it to them, saying, This is My body which is being given for you; do this in remembrance of Me" (Luke 22:19). The Lord did not tell the disciples that at the Lord's table they had to quiet their hearts to meditate on Him in remembrance of Him. Rather, the Lord said, "This is My body which is being given for you; do this in remembrance of Me." What the Lord indicated was that to remember Him is to eat Him. The remembrance in the Bible is not meditating. First and foremost, it is eating. What do we eat? We eat the Lord's body.

Verse 20 continues, "And similarly the cup after they had dined, saying, This cup is the new covenant established in My blood, which is being poured out for you." The Lord meant that He wanted them to drink the cup in remembrance of Him. Hence, what is a remembrance of the Lord? We remember the Lord when we eat the Lord's body and drink the Lord's blood. The remembrance of the Lord in the Bible is to eat and drink the Lord. To remember the Lord is to eat the Lord's body and drink the Lord's blood.

THE LORD BECOMING OUR FOOD

What does it mean to eat the Lord's body and drink the Lord's blood? To eat the Lord's body and drink His blood is to eat and drink of the Lord Himself. A person may say, "I have eaten some chicken." How was he able to eat the chicken? Without death and without the shedding of blood, the chicken could not have entered into him. The reason that the Lord Jesus can enter into us and become our food is that He died and shed His blood.

One day the Lord Jesus told the Jews, "Work not for the food which perishes, but for the food which abides unto eternal life, which the Son of Man will give you" (John 6:27). This meant that the Jews should not seek to eat bread and be filled, because bread is merely physical food and temporary. Instead, they should seek the food that abides unto eternal life. The bread that the Lord would give was His flesh, but the Jews did not understand Him. As a result, they contended with one another, saying, "How can this man give us His flesh to eat?" (v. 52). Then the Lord Jesus said, "He who eats My flesh and drinks My blood has eternal life...For My flesh is true food, and My blood is true drink. He who eats My flesh and drinks My blood abides in Me and I in him" (vv. 54-56). Then many of His disciples said, "This word is hard; who can hear it?" (v. 60). This was because they were full of their natural concepts.

What is it to eat the Lord's flesh and drink the Lord's blood? To eat the Lord's flesh and drink His blood is to take the Lord into us by eating and drinking Him. The Lord is life. Therefore, when He comes into us, eternal life comes into us.

EATING AND DRINKING THE LORD
BEING TO RECEIVE THE LORD

From this we see that through His death the Lord gave Himself to us. If He had not died or shed His blood, He could not have any relationship with us and would not have a way to enter into us. He can enter into us because He died and shed His blood and thus became edible and drinkable to us. Now whenever we turn to our spirit, believing and receiving the Lord who died and shed His blood for us, we eat His flesh and drink His blood. We believe that in His body He bore our sins on the cross, that He died for us, and that His blood was shed for us on the cross. In God's eyes, when we believe and receive the Lord in this way, we are eating His flesh and drinking His blood.

What was accomplished through the Lord's flesh and blood is now our portion. When we believe in Him and receive Him, He enters into us through the Holy Spirit. When this happens, He is in us and in union with us, and we are in Him and in union with Him. Thus, to eat the Lord's flesh and drink the Lord's blood is to receive the Lord Himself as our enjoyment, our life within, and our food. This is to eat the Lord's flesh and drink the Lord's blood.

The greatest principle in eating and drinking is receiving, and the principle in receiving is union. Whatever we eat and whatever we drink will enter into us. Moreover, we are united with what we eat and drink. No matter how much we meditate on a person, he cannot come into us. Hence, bread breaking is not to meditate on the Lord but to eat the Lord's body and drink His blood. In baptism we enter into Christ and are united with Christ, and in bread breaking we eat and drink the Lord Himself and are thus united and mingled with Him. Every time we break the bread, more of the Lord comes into us. Every time we remember the Lord, we have a deeper union with the Lord. This is to remember the Lord.

EATING, DRINKING, AND
REMEMBERING THE LORD IN SPIRIT

In the past when we remembered the Lord, many of our concepts were religious and much of our remembrance was in our mind. Every time we came to the Lord's table, we contemplated His being God, His becoming flesh, His living on the earth for thirty-three and a half years, His dying on the cross, His being raised in three days, His ascending to the throne, and His waiting to come again. We always remembered the Lord in this way—we worshipped and meditated on Him in our mind. However, the Lord said that He is Spirit and that those who worship Him must worship in spirit and truthfulness (4:24). Only when we use our spirit and are in our spirit can we touch the Lord, worship the Lord, and genuinely remember the Lord.

Genuine remembrance of the Lord is receiving the Lord and allowing Him to enter into us again. The Lord said, "This is My body which is being given for you; do this in remembrance of Me...This cup is the new covenant established in My blood, which is being poured out for you" (Luke 22:19-20). We eat the bread, which signifies the Lord's body, and drink the cup, which signifies the Lord's blood. We do this in remembrance of the Lord. Our eating and drinking of the Lord is our remembrance of the Lord. The Lord does not want us to meditate on Him or contact Him with our mind; rather, the Lord wants us to contact Him, eat Him, and drink Him with our spirit. When He was broken for us on the cross, He shed His blood and released His life. The bread and cup that we touch outwardly signify His body that was given for us and His blood that was shed for us. This means that He has died and His life has been released from within Him. Now we not only receive the visible bread and cup outwardly, but at the same time, we also touch and receive the Lord Himself in our spirit. We allow Him to come into us afresh, and again we gain Him, receive Him, and enjoy Him. The Lord said that this is to be "in remembrance of Me."

REMEMBERING THE LORD
BEING TO RECEIVE THE LORD ANEW

In breaking bread, when we see the symbols, we turn to our spirit and receive the Lord again and again. Every time we break bread, we receive the Lord anew, and every time we break bread, we again contact the Lord who died and resurrected, touching Him in our spirit. If we truly see this, the next time we break bread, we will realize that inwardly we have been filled with many other things so that the Lord is not able to find any place, any empty room, in us. When we realize this, we need to pray, "O Lord, remove all the things that should not be in me so that You may have a place in me." The revelation we see will expose our inward problems and cause us to tell the Lord spontaneously, "O Lord, I am glad to pour myself out and empty myself. O Lord, I receive You as the Spirit into me. Fill me with Your resurrection life." By doing this, we will definitely be filled with Christ after breaking the bread.

There was once a brother who had been at odds with his wife for a long time. Inwardly, he felt that this was not right, but he simply could not help it. Every time he came to the Lord's table, after singing a hymn and calming down, he would begin to pray, "Lord, You are God, who took the form of a sinner and humbled Yourself for us. You were born in

Bethlehem, grew up in Nazareth..." He enjoyed his prayer, and the saints were joyful in their spirits. However, just as he was unhappy with his wife before the Lord's table, he was unhappy with her after the meeting also. After the Lord's table and after this meditation and prayer in his mind, he still had not been touched by the Lord inwardly. Therefore, he was the same after the meeting as he was before the meeting. He was still intact and was the same as he had always been.

One day, however, after receiving revelation and seeing that remembrance of the Lord is actually to receive the Lord, he could not touch the bread anymore. Why was he unable to do this? He could not touch the bread because he realized that since he was not pleased with his wife, he could not receive Christ within even though he might take the bread outwardly. Thus, he could no longer break the bread. Because he felt very wrong, he prayed, pouring out his sins and everything that was in him, saying, "O Lord, I pour out all my displeasure, my self, my sins, and the world that is within me." This was not a meditation in the mind but an inward receiving of the Lord. In that one hour of remembering the Lord by breaking bread, he enjoyed the Lord again. As a result, he became a different person.

BREAKING BREAD BEING
TO PARTAKE OF THE LORD'S TABLE

The Bible tells us that when we break bread, we partake of the Lord's table (1 Cor. 10:16-17, 21) and enjoy the Lord. When we invite people for a meal, we cannot serve ourselves as food. However, the Lord's table is different. In the Lord's table the Lord Himself is spread on the table. What is spread on the Lord's table is the Lord Himself. In remembering the Lord we come to His table, and on this table His flesh and blood are displayed. Today Christianity has made the Lord's table a religious matter, without the reality of Christ. However, when we come to the Lord's table, we come to receive the Lord Himself. We empty ourselves so that the Lord can come in. In this one hour we enjoy the Lord by eating and drinking of Him. By the end we have received and enjoyed Him inwardly. As a result, the world and the flesh are gone.

To partake of the Lord's table is to remember the Lord. Is there anyone who would attend a feast merely to observe and think but not to eat and drink? Everyone who attends a feast surely eats and drinks. Thus, if we truly know what it means to remember the Lord, we will definitely eat and drink to our heart's content at the Lord's table. Then every time we remember the Lord, we will be able to say with boldness that all of our hunger and thirst are fully satisfied. When people ask us about what we are eating and drinking, we can tell them readily that we are eating and drinking the Lord Jesus. When we receive Him into us, He becomes our life and strength within, enabling us to love those whom we cannot love, to do what we cannot do, to be what we cannot be, and to live in a way that we cannot live. Then during the week He will be digested in us to become our everything, making us joyful and satisfied. This is to enjoy Christ and to receive the Lord.

I hope that our remembrance of the Lord will not be centered on meditating but will be based upon receiving. Every time we remember Him, may we eat Him, drink Him, and enjoy Him inwardly. Then may we take His riches back with us so that we will have Him as our satisfaction, joy, and supply. This is to remember the Lord.

CHAPTER TWO

THE LEADING IN THE MEETINGS

THE IMPORTANCE OF MEETINGS

Many Christians do not understand the reason they need to meet, but meetings are of supreme importance to Christians. History shows that meeting is a characteristic of the church. Prior to the existence of the church, mankind did not understand the value and function of meetings. It was not until the church was produced that men came to know the significance of meeting together, because meeting together enables men to accomplish many things that they otherwise could not.

In the Old Testament age, even before the church was produced, God's people lived a meeting life. In the Bible the unique God called the children of Israel an assembly. They had to assemble together when they worshipped God and listened to His instruction. God gathered them together when He was ready to perform a great thing. During the forty years in the wilderness, they lived a life of assembling together. After they entered Canaan, the good land, they continued to follow God's command and gather in Jerusalem at least three times a year to worship God corporately by keeping the Feast of Passover (the Feast of Unleavened Bread), the Feast of Pentecost, and the Feast of Tabernacles. When they gathered together, either the priests or the prophets would instruct them according to the teachings of God. Great or important matters among them were also decided in such gatherings. After the children of Israel returned from their captivity, Ezra gathered them together and read the law to them (Ezra 7:10; Neh. 8). God's people gathered together even in heavy rain to deal with their transgression against God until the whole matter was resolved (Ezra 10:7-14). Hence, the meeting life is a service of the church.

In the Gospel of Matthew the Lord Jesus mentioned the church twice: one time concerning the foundation of the church and another time concerning the church life. In chapter 16 we see that the foundation of the church is Christ as the rock (v. 18). Then in chapter 18, concerning the church life, the Lord said, "For where there are two or three gathered into My name, there am I in their midst" (v. 20). In the same chapter He also said that if an offending brother refuses to hear the brothers' reproof, the brothers should tell it to the church (vv. 15-17). Thus, chapter 18 is on the church life.

In Acts when the church was ready to be brought forth as a child being delivered from a mother's womb, one hundred twenty people gathered daily in the Lord's presence to pray in one accord (1:13-15; 2:1). The church was produced through the gathering of the saints. After the church came into existence, those in the church gathered together every day. Later they brought three thousand and then another five thousand to salvation. They lived the church life together (2:41-42, 46-47; 4:4; 5:42). The Greek word for *church* is *ekklesia,* meaning "a called-out congregation." In Chinese the term was rendered as *jiao hui,* meaning "a religious gathering." This is a poor translation, because the church is not a religious gathering but an *ekklesia,* a gathering of the called-out ones.

The meaning of the word *church* can be clearly seen in the type of the children of Israel. When the Israelites were scattered in Egypt, God called them out into the wilderness to become an assembly. Even though there was no such title as the *church,* the gathering of those called out by God was the church, the assembly. The church life is a meeting life, an assembling life. Hebrews 10:25 says, "Not abandoning our own assembling together." Meeting together is the greatest, most practical, and most effective way for Christians to be built up. Meetings are extremely important to the Christian life.

A good meeting can be of tremendous help to a Christian, and a poor meeting can cause much harm to a Christian.

Whether or not we are edified in our spiritual life hinges on the meetings of our local church. It is in the meetings that we can receive much edification and spiritual help. Although we receive benefits from praying to God, reading the Bible, and fellowshipping with God individually, and even from fellowshipping with the saints, none of these benefits can be compared with the benefit we receive in the meetings. If the meetings are poor, we will suffer a great loss. Sometimes a meeting might not seem poor, but if the Lord's work, the Lord's presence, and the Spirit's moving are not present, it is a loss to the brothers and sisters.

A saint once shared his feeling with me, saying, "If I do not come to the meeting, I have no peace; however, if I come, I feel burdened." The meetings are for worshipping and serving God. If our meetings are burdensome, we need to correct and adjust the meetings so that the saints do not suffer loss. If a meeting does not have the presence of the Holy Spirit, the saints will feel that the time is going by slowly, but if a meeting is full of the presence of the Holy Spirit, they will sense that the meeting goes by quickly. All the Lord's workers and responsible ones in the church should pay attention to the matter of how to lead a meeting so that the brothers and sisters will benefit and not suffer loss.

HOW TO LEAD A MEETING

Entering into Fellowship with the Lord before the Meeting

The prerequisite of leading a meeting is that we must first enter into fellowship with the Lord. If we are not in fellowship with the Lord, a meeting will bring in burden and death. For example, if no one at a Lord's table meeting has entered into fellowship with the Lord, all of our elements of death will be combined when we are together, and the resulting death in the meeting will be unimaginable. We will bring in death if we have not entered into fellowship with the Lord before coming to a meeting. If this is the case, no one may have selected a hymn and no prayers may have been offered even five minutes after the scheduled time for the meeting to begin. This is altogether a dead situation. The Lord's table meeting is a real test to the condition of our spirit. If everyone's spirit is deadened and quiet in a Lord's table meeting, and no one has chosen a hymn or prayed, the responsible brothers may feel compelled to choose a hymn. But eventually, the more we sing, the more we will feel deadened and depressed. After the meeting someone might say, "The meeting today was really poor; it was very bad." A young one might say, "I am not coming next time." Who then is responsible for the meeting? We are all responsible. Hence, the prerequisite for leading a meeting is that we must all first enter into fellowship with the Lord. Then we can meet in the Spirit of the Lord.

If we all meet in this way, the meetings will issue in life and the living Spirit. However, if we meet outside of the fellowship with the Lord, the meetings will bring in death. In a meeting of four hundred people, if there are forty who live in fellowship with the Lord, allow the Holy Spirit to operate in them, and serve as channels of the Holy Spirit, that meeting will be uplifted and enriched. In order to enter into fellowship with the Lord, we need to touch His presence through dealings, prayer, and fellowship with Him prior to our coming to a meeting. In this way we will be enlivened, and others will be affected. Some saints have learned to live in the Lord and in the Spirit. When they enter a meeting, they bring the Spirit and life to the meeting. Thus, we should never take the meetings lightly, thinking that we can come in a casual way without living in fellowship with the Lord. We need to know that the prerequisite of leading a meeting is to enter into fellowship with the Lord and then enter a meeting in the spirit of fellowship.

Touching the Spirit of the Meeting

Before we come to a meeting, we must enter into fellowship with the Lord. But once we enter a meeting, the first thing we must do is to touch the spirit of the meeting. For example, everyone at a wedding meeting is full of joy. But if two children are crying and making noise, some will say that they are not proper. Whenever we enter a meeting, we need to touch the atmosphere and spirit of the meeting in a spirit of fellowship. Every meeting, or every kind of meeting, has its spirit. If our spirit is living and sensitive, we will be able to touch the spirit of a meeting. For instance, we should not be singing, "Praise Him! praise Him! praise the Savior!" when we enter a memorial meeting. We should not be those who are without feeling or sensitivity. If the atmosphere of the meeting is sorrowful, we should be able to touch that spirit once we step into the meeting, and immediately feel sorrowful. Even if we were praising the Lord on our way to the meeting, once we enter into the mournful atmosphere of the meeting, our inner feeling should be sorrowful.

The problem with many saints is that they neither care for the spirit of the meeting nor touch the atmosphere of the meeting. It is as if whatever is happening in the meeting has nothing to do with them. They are all smiles while someone is weeping in prayer. They do not care for the spirit of the meeting; instead, they are concerned only for their feeling. For example, in a table meeting the spirit of the meeting may cause everyone to sense the Lord's dignity and greatness. Then a brother, unaware of the spirit and the atmosphere of the meeting, may select an irrelevant hymn as he enters the meeting. Because he has been singing and contemplating this hymn every day at home, he selects the hymn when he enters the meeting, regardless of the atmosphere of the meeting. He cares only for his feeling. Selecting hymns in this way is like laughing at a memorial meeting.

When we enter a meeting, we must touch the atmosphere, the spirit, of the meeting. We must put aside our personal feeling and be sensitive to touch the atmosphere of the meeting by the spirit of fellowship. We should do this in the Lord's table meeting, the prayer meeting, the fellowship meeting, and the meeting for the ministry of the word. For instance, we may have prepared a message to give in a meeting, but when we enter the meeting, we may touch an atmosphere that is not in line with the message we prepared. We should drop the original message and speak another message. Sometimes when we are talking with others, we must drop what we intended to say because the atmosphere is inappropriate. At that moment we need to observe the countenances of others, touch their feelings, and then speak accordingly. In conclusion, when we come to a meeting, we must exercise our living spirit within to touch the spirit and atmosphere of the meeting. Only when we have inwardly touched the atmosphere do we have anything to express, either by selecting a hymn or offering a prayer. We must always touch the feeling of a meeting with our spirit.

Preparing Ourselves and Opening Our Spirit So That the Holy Spirit Has a Channel

Before we come to a meeting we must enter into fellowship with the Lord. Then as we enter a meeting we must touch the spirit of the meeting. Furthermore, we must prepare ourselves and open our spirit so that the Holy Spirit can use us as a channel to speak for Him. However, some saints have made up their mind before coming to a meeting that they will not open their mouth, because they want only to attend a meeting and to listen to a message. They are determined to merely listen. This is because they think that the prayer meeting is for the praying ones to pray and the ministry meeting is for the ministering ones to minister; therefore, they come to listen. This is wrong. We should not have this kind of thought. We should open our spirit and allow the Holy Spirit to use us as a channel to speak for Him.

No Order in the Lord's Table Meeting

In some localities the responsible brothers always sit in the front at the Lord's table meeting. We cannot find this in the Bible. There are only brothers at the table meeting; there are no responsible brothers. The primary reason the responsible brothers sit in the first row should be for the convenience of making announcements. I am afraid, however, that the responsible brothers have the concept that they are responsible for leading the table meeting. We need to be clear that no one should be taking the lead in the table meeting. Strictly speaking, there should be no particular seating arrangement at the Lord's table. For example, sometimes I sit at the front in the meeting; at other times I sit with a younger brother. In this way, the saints have the impression that there is no special seating at the Lord's table: I am a slave of God and a brother to them.

The saints must be clear that there is no special seating in the Lord's table meeting. Otherwise, ten years from now, all the elders will be sitting in the front row and will consider that they are leading the meeting. All the responsible brothers should realize that there is no special order established by men. Any order established by men is erroneous. Brother George Müller of England sat at the very back in every Lord's table meeting. Although that was quite good, some might have the impression that it was too much. When we come to the Lord's table, we should not have a concept regarding who should sit at the front and who should sit at the back. The new believers, the newly saved ones, should sit at the front with those who have been saved for a longer time. For example, if there are four children in a family, the youngest would always sit next to the father at mealtimes. This is the order in a family. Breaking of bread, being a family matter, should also keep the same order.

Not Replacing the Saints

In the churches in Taiwan, the opening and closing of the meetings, whether at the Lord's table, prayer, or fellowship meeting, are done by responsible brothers. Almost every time, one of the responsible brothers selects a hymn at the beginning of the meeting, and then everyone else joins in to sing. Imperceptibly, it seems that only the responsible brothers are priests. However, in the New Testament age we are all priests. The saints in all the churches should be clear concerning this. The co-workers, elders, and ones responsible for the home meetings should avoid selecting hymns at the beginning of the table meeting, prayer meeting, and fellowship meeting in order to not replace the priestly function of the saints. In addition, they should not conclude the meeting for the saints. Among us there should be an atmosphere of "not replacing." All the saints should participate and function in the meetings. The leading ones among us should not nullify the spirit of the brothers and sisters by serving as priests on their behalf. May the Lord have mercy on the churches so that the leading ones will not be the only ones responsible for beginning and ending the meetings but that all the saints would function in this way.

The responsible brothers in all the localities should avoid replacing the saints in selecting hymns at the beginning of a meeting. Any saint can select a hymn according to the moving of the Spirit. In this matter the sisters are not excluded; they can also pray and sing according to the moving of the Spirit. The responsible brothers should never be the only ones to take care of the beginning and ending of a meeting. The responsible brothers are responsible for the administration of the church, that is, to take the lead in administrating the church. However, at the table meeting all the saints come together before the Lord. Moreover, blessing the bread and the cup should not be done exclusively by the responsible brothers. Rather, the responsible brothers should perfect the newly saved ones to bless the bread and the cup. For example, we can begin to perfect a brother who was saved and baptized yesterday to bless the bread and the cup and to pass them to the saints at the table meeting.

If a father assigns the youngest child to distribute some candy to everyone in the family, there will be a sense of sweetness; however, the feeling will not be as sweet if the father assigns the oldest brother to distribute the candy. At the Lord's supper, the Lord said to His disciples, "Take, eat…Drink of it, all of you" (Matt. 26:26-27). There is no reference to Peter being at the front. Hence, especially in the Lord's table meeting, we should not have a set order. At the end of the Lord's table meeting a responsible brother can stand up and make the announcements concerning the move of the church. During the Lord's table meeting there are no responsible brothers; everyone is a brother. If we are not clear in this matter, the meeting will not have a good beginning. All the brothers and sisters will focus on the responsible brothers, thinking that the responsible brothers should be the first to select a hymn and pray. This will quench the spirit of the meeting. Before God we do not have any order in the Lord's table meeting. Before we come to the meeting, we must enter into fellowship with the Lord; in the meeting we must touch the feeling of the spirit and select hymns according to the inspiration of the Spirit. After singing we should all pray, testify, or speak.

SELECTING HYMNS IN A MEETING

After a meeting begins, once we touch the spirit of the meeting, we will begin to function. Let us now speak concerning selecting hymns. Do not consider this to be an ordinary matter. Selecting hymns in a meeting involves many details. In order to select hymns we need knowledge in two aspects. First, we must know the hymn categories: some hymns are for praising, some for prayer, some for spiritual warfare, some for edification, some for gospel preaching, some for touching the Spirit, some for remembering the Lord, and some for worshipping the Father. We must have knowledge of the different categories of the hymns if we want to select proper hymns in a meeting. Otherwise, we are likely to make mistakes in selecting hymns. Second, we must understand the progression of the meeting. This may be likened to the four seasons of the year. For each season we wear clothes of different thickness. We dress lightly in summer, warmer in fall, and the warmest in winter. Likewise, the hymns we select in a meeting should be altogether according to the atmosphere and course of the meeting. Therefore, in selecting hymns, we must be clear concerning the different categories of hymns and also know the atmosphere and progression of a meeting.

DIFFERENT HYMNS TO BE USED
IN THE COURSE OF A MEETING

In the entire course of a meeting we need different hymns for different sections of a meeting. For example, we may have ten kinds of hymns to meet the need of different sections of the meeting. The first hymn should be an opening hymn. After the opening hymn we should lead the saints into the subject of the meeting. Hence, the second hymn should be an introductory hymn that brings the entire meeting to its central subject. Sometimes, if there may not have been a strong release of the spirit of a hymn, there is the need for a third kind of hymn, a strengthening hymn. At such a time we need to strengthen the spirit. But if the strengthening hymn is not sufficient, we will need a fourth kind of hymn that can uplift the spirit. However, a hymn for uplifting the spirit does not necessarily have to follow a strengthening hymn. A fifth kind of hymn is a turning hymn. When someone selects the wrong hymn and the singing begins to drag, there is the need to turn by selecting another hymn. For example, in a meeting where everyone senses the Lord's greatness and exaltedness, a brother may select a gospel hymn. At such a time there is the need for someone to select another hymn immediately. A sixth kind of hymn, similar to a turning hymn, is a correcting hymn. For example, someone may select a hymn about praising the Lord after the bread and cup have been passed. At this time someone should correct this choice by selecting a hymn related to the worship of the Father. A seventh kind of hymn maintains the spirit. If the meeting has not reached its conclusion, there is the need to maintain the spirit of the meeting. An eighth kind of hymn fills the gap and adjusts the length of a meeting. Sometimes if the meeting is too long and needs some adjustment, someone can adjust it with a hymn. The ninth kind of hymn is a concluding hymn, and the tenth kind of hymn is a lingering hymn, a hymn for lingering before sending people off. Sometimes a meeting has ended, yet it seems that the meeting is still not over; at such times there is the need for a "sending off" hymn. This is based on Genesis 18. When Abraham was reluctant to let Jehovah go, he walked a distance with Him to send Him off (v. 16).

An opening hymn serves two purposes. First, it calms the saints' hearts. Often our hearts are not settled when we walk into a meeting. The singing of a hymn can calm our hearts. Second, an opening hymn allows time for all the saints to arrive. The second hymn should bring the saints' hearts into the central subject of a meeting. In short, because the first hymn is for the preparation of the saints' hearts, the singing should be living. But we should not go too high too fast; rather, we should sing verse by verse to calm the saints' hearts so that they may be brought into the presence of God. Hence, no matter what kind of meeting we are in, we can select a longer hymn for the first one. The second hymn brings the saints into the central subject of a meeting, leading them into the spirit of a meeting.

Suppose in a prayer meeting we sense that the atmosphere is for the spreading of the gospel; we should not select a hymn that does not have the flavor of prayer. Even though a hymn of encouragement can be used in ministering the Word or in encouraging the brothers and sisters to preach the gospel, it is not appropriate in a prayer meeting. Therefore, if we select the wrong hymn, it will be difficult to go on in the meeting. If we are not familiar with the hymns and expect to be inspired by the Holy Spirit, we are waiting for a miracle. Hence, a knowledge of the hymns and the selection of hymns are very important.

An opening hymn should be long enough for the spirit of the saints to be fanned into flame. If a hymn is not long enough, the saints will not be sufficiently "pumped up" in their spirit; they will be like those who are out of breath when they run home from the street and go directly to the dining table. In order for the opening hymn to stir up and uplift the spirit of the saints, the tune must be powerful, and it must be easy to sing; moreover, the lyrics should be of adequate length. For instance, *Hymns,* #213 is a good hymn for beginning the table meeting. If all the brothers and sisters sense that the Lord is full of glory and honor, then they can sing *Hymns,* #127, and continue with *Hymns,* #183. To do this, however, we must have some spiritual skill, and the spirit of the meeting must also be able to keep pace. Otherwise, as a rule, after singing *Hymns,* #127, we will not be able to find another hymn as a continuation because the singing has already reached the peak. For this reason we might need to reserve *Hymns,* #127 for later and sing *Hymns,* #183 first. However, if we are experienced in spirit and realize that even though *Hymns,* #127 is high, it cannot fully express our inner feeling; then perhaps we can continue with *Hymns,* #141. In such an uplifted spirit we can break the bread to remember the Lord, singing, "Jesus, Thy head, once crown'd with thorns, / Is crown'd with glory now; / Heaven's royal diadem adorns / The mighty Victor's brow" (stanza 1). If we all remember the

Lord in this way, the brothers and sisters will receive an unimaginable supply.

I hope that the responsible brothers in the various localities will bring this matter to the Lord and learn to put it into practice. Otherwise, although we may give people food in our meetings, we may cause them to have indigestion. Meetings are for the edification of the saints, but if we do not know how to meet in a proper way, we will not only fail to edify the saints but also ruin their spiritual appetite. If we begin a meeting with *Hymns,* #183, continue with *Hymns,* #127, follow with an uplifted blessing, and then go on to *Hymns,* #141, the saints will surely feel comfortable and receive nourishment.

SEVERAL MATTERS THAT REQUIRE OUR ATTENTION

We all need to be serious and familiarize ourselves with the hymns. We should even memorize some of the hymns. The leading brothers, in particular, must spend time in this matter; otherwise, their work will be meaningless. Some of the leading brothers may say that they have a blueprint in their hand, yet after a while what they are attempting to carry out may become dead and full of the flesh. If so, there is a problem. Therefore, we need to have a careful consideration concerning the blueprint. Sometimes a blueprint may not be entirely accurate, so it is best that the brothers do not design a blueprint by themselves; rather, they should do it in coordination with the saints. Even if we have a correct blueprint, however, our way and method may not be right. Sometimes we lead the saints to consecrate themselves and to begin with their spirit, but we have not led them to deal with sins. This is not appropriate. The Holy Spirit never works together with the flesh. Thus, if we work by the flesh, we are finished. We must all learn this lesson: once we touch the Lord's work, we must learn to reject and deal with our flesh.

CHAPTER THREE

BEARING RESPONSIBILITY FOR THE MEETING

First Corinthians 14:23-26 says, "If therefore the whole church comes together in one place,...indeed God is among you...Whenever you come together, each one has a psalm, has a teaching, has a revelation, has a tongue, has an interpretation. Let all things be done for building up." This shows the proper situation of a normal church meeting.

THE IMPORTANCE OF MEETINGS

Strictly speaking, the Christian life is a meeting life. Much of the grace a Christian receives is in the meetings, and much of the work the Lord does is also in the meetings. Matthew 18:20 says, "For where there are two or three gathered into My name, there am I in their midst." Moreover, Hebrews 10:25 says, "Not abandoning our own assembling together." Since the Christian life is a meeting life and much of the Lord's work is carried out through the meetings, we must regard Christian meetings as an important matter.

PRAYING FOR AND VISITING THE SAINTS

We need to pray for the brothers and sisters in our small group meeting and visit them. It would be best if we could prepare a prayer record, with the names of the saints in our group. We should pray for at least one person each day and cover everyone in the group every week. This is worthwhile. At the same time, based on our burden, we can fellowship with them in order to gain a better understanding of their situation. Then we can pray for them to have a heart for the Lord, and we can help them fulfill their desire and goal toward the Lord. Therefore, prayer is of supreme importance, and it is very effective. In addition to praying for the saints, we can also fellowship and talk with them before and after the meetings. If the Lord leads, we can even visit them during the week. We may also write them to share what we have heard and enjoyed in the meetings, thereby keeping in touch with them. We should be diligent in these matters before the Lord. If every brother and sister is willing to do these things, they are doing a good work that is valuable in the Lord's sight and acceptable to God.

LEARNING TO BEAR RESPONSIBILITY FOR THE MEETINGS

Besides praying for and fellowshipping with the saints, in the church life we should also learn to bear responsibility for the meetings. It will be difficult for a meeting to have the rich presence of the Lord if we do not bear responsibility for the meeting by exercising our spirit and living according to the spirit. If the Holy Spirit cannot find channels in a meeting, the saints whom we bring to the meeting will not be moved or benefited. Eventually, after one or two meetings they will no longer come. This will be a big loss to them, and a great loss to the church. The brothers and sisters in a small group meeting must see that they should not only pray for those in their group and fellowship with them, but they should also learn to bear responsibility along with the elders for the meetings.

In Christianity, pastors and preachers take the lead and are responsible for the meetings. Everyone who has been to a "Sunday service" in the denominations knows that there are pastors who lead the meetings. Arrangements are made beforehand as to who will choose the hymns, who will lead the singing, who will be the first to pray, who will be the second to pray, and so forth. The rest of the believers are merely spectators; they watch what others do and listen to what others say, but they themselves do not bear any responsibility for the meeting. This is not scriptural. This may be practiced in a gospel meeting or a message meeting. However, to practice this in the Lord's table, fellowship, and prayer meetings is altogether contrary to the nature of meetings as revealed in the Bible. All the saints should come together and follow the leading of the Holy Spirit for the Lord's table, fellowship, and prayer meetings. As described in 1 Corinthians 14, some may have a psalm, a teaching, or a revelation; we should function according to the spirit so that others will see that God is indeed among us (v. 25). This kind of church meeting is a meeting according to the Scriptures.

Meetings for preaching the gospel or for ministering the word may be taken care of by a few brothers. But when the whole church is gathered together for exhortation or for the exercise of gifts, all the saints should participate by following the spirit within. The brothers and sisters should follow the spirit to bear the burden and responsibility for the meeting; otherwise, it will be like coming to a hall of worship to merely attend a meeting and to let the pastors lead the meeting. We must know that if we do not bear the burden for the Lord's table, fellowship, and prayer meetings, it will be difficult for the newly saved ones to begin a meeting.

For example, at the Lord's table meeting, if none of the elders or responsible brothers who are sitting in the front row select a hymn, the meeting will not begin. This shows that we are not bearing the responsibility for the meeting. If the elders would not call a hymn, we would simply sit there. It is as if we are behaving as guests invited to a meal instead of cooking it. A meeting should not have to wait for a responsible brother to call a hymn before it can begin. Where does this practice come from? It comes from our unwillingness to bear responsibility for the meetings.

Never think that the first two rows are reserved for responsible brothers, elders, and deacons. When we come to a meeting to pray and worship God, we all have an equal standing; we are all brothers and sisters. Sometimes for convenience in the service, the brother who makes announcements may sit in the front, but this is not always necessary. The elders can scatter themselves among the other brothers, sitting with them before God. When it is time to begin the meeting, all the brothers should bear the responsibility for selecting hymns, thereby sharing the burden of the meeting.

If the elders and responsible brothers would not take the lead, the whole meeting will be left without anyone to bear the burden. This indicates that we have problems. According to the principle in 1 Corinthians 14, all of the brothers and sisters should bear responsibility. In this way, the saints who are newly saved will see that the meeting belongs to everyone and not merely to the elders or a few responsible brothers. Spontaneously, they will also pick up this responsibility. Thus, we all have a great responsibility in the meetings.

If we are in a small group meeting, we should share the burden. We should all select hymns and pray. Then all the saints who attend the meeting will realize that the meeting is not merely the responsibility of a few responsible brothers but of all the saints. Thus, it is easy to carry on the meeting in a healthy way.

HOW TO BEAR RESPONSIBILITY IN THE MEETING

Having Fellowship with the Lord

How can we bear responsibility in a meeting? How can we exercise our spirit in a meeting? To bear responsibility in a meeting, we must first prepare our spirit and have fellowship with the Lord. If we do not have fellowship with the Lord before coming to a meeting, our spirit will be deadened and lack vitality. If this is the case, it will be difficult for us to bear the burden in a meeting. To bear the burden in a meeting, we must have personal fellowship with the Lord for our spirit to be uplifted.

Being Fully Open to the Lord and to the Meeting

Second, when we come to a meeting, we must learn to fully open ourselves to the Lord and to the meeting. This affords the Holy Spirit the opportunity to use us and to touch us. This also enables us to sense the atmosphere and flavor of the meeting so that we know which hymn to select and how to pray. Therefore, we must be open in the meetings and be ready to receive the burden from the Holy Spirit. Many brothers and sisters do not prepare themselves before a meeting. They do not remember that there is a meeting until ten minutes before the meeting begins. Then they hurriedly rush to the meeting without bearing any burden for the meeting and their spirit is still closed. Then at the meeting only a few brothers will take care of the meeting to select hymns and pray; they are like priests for the church who minister on behalf of the saints. Although this is not prearranged, every attendant knows that someone will select a hymn and someone will pray; everyone else can simply sit, watch, and do nothing because a few brothers will bear the full responsibility. Since a few brothers will take the lead to select a hymn and to pray, the rest of the saints can relax and enjoy. We should never be like this. Prior to any meeting we should open our spirit. After we sit down in the meeting, we should seek the Lord as to what He desires us to do. We must touch the feeling of the Holy Spirit and receive inspiration from Him. If we are open in this way, the Holy Spirit will surely move us to receive the burden.

Touching the Atmosphere of the Meeting

Third, upon entering a meeting we must learn to touch the atmosphere, the spirit, of the meeting. Suppose a brother was taken by the Lord, and the saints are holding a memorial meeting in his home. When we enter the house, we can sense a sorrowful atmosphere; we can touch a sorrowful spirit. It would be inappropriate for us to laugh and select any hymn we please. Conversely, if we are in a wedding meeting, where the atmosphere is joyful, it would be unfitting for us to ignore the atmosphere, the spirit, of the meeting and select a hymn that asks for the Lord's mercy.

When we come into a meeting, we should be prepared in spirit, our entire being should be open to the Lord and to the meeting, and we should exercise our spirit to touch the atmosphere of the meeting. Then we will be a channel for the Holy Spirit, and He will be able to use us as a channel to bear responsibility for the meeting.

A TWOFOLD KNOWLEDGE NEEDED FOR SELECTING HYMNS

Concerning the selection of hymns, we need a twofold knowledge. First, we need to know the hymns in their categories; second, we need to know the progression of singing in a meeting. According to categories, there are hymns on preaching the gospel, prayer, spiritual pursuit, spiritual edification, spiritual warfare, praise, bread breaking, and worship. We must be familiar with all the categories. Otherwise, we may touch the Lord's presence and sense His glory yet select a hymn on rising up to preach the gospel. This would not be fitting, and it would not be proper. For this reason, we must spend time to study our hymns.

We must also know the progression of singing in a meeting. In a table meeting, the first hymn is a beginning hymn, which should be longer in order to calm the saints' hearts and bring the saints to the Lord. Because a meeting has a beginning section, there are beginning hymns.

THE PROGRESSION OF A MEETING

There are roughly ten steps in the progression of a meeting. The first step is the opening, and the second is the introduction which brings the meeting to its subject. After an opening hymn is sung and a strong prayer is offered, the second hymn should bring the meeting to its subject. After the saints sing the introductory hymn, there should be some introductory prayers concerning the subject. The third step is the strengthening. If the meeting is still not strong after singing and prayers related to the first and second steps, there will be a need to call another hymn, a strengthening hymn. If the spirit is still not strong enough after singing the strengthening hymn and offering some strong prayers, there will be a need for the fourth step, which is the stirring up of the spirit. Sometimes the third and fourth steps transpire simultaneously.

The fifth step is the turning. For example, after the remembrance of the Lord, we need to turn to worship the Father. Sometimes the Lord's table has not reached the point of worshipping the Father, but a brother selects *Hymns,* #33; sometimes a brother selects *Hymns,* #101 immediately after the bread and the cup have been passed. Both are inappropriate. Hence, there is the need of a sixth step for correction. Sometimes a meeting may be quite long. For example, when a great number of saints gather together, it may take a longer time for the bread and the cup to be passed. If this is the case, there may be the need to maintain the spirit through a hymn or some prayers. This is the seventh step, maintaining the spirit for the meeting. Even though we use hymns and prayers to maintain the spirit, there may still be the need to fill up the time with more prayers and singing. This is the eighth step. Then toward the end of the meeting comes the ninth step to sing a concluding hymn. Sometimes even though the meeting has ended, there is still a lingering air; thus, we may select another hymn to send the saints off. This is the tenth step. This can be compared to sending off a friend who has visited you by walking a distance with him.

We often have the sense at the end of the Lord's table meeting that everyone wishes the meeting could continue. At such a time, without waiting for the brothers to call a hymn, everyone may spontaneously begin to sing, "Glory, honor, praise and power, / Be unto the Lamb forever! / Jesus Christ is our Redeemer, / Hallelujah! Hallelujah! / Hallelujah! Praise ye the Lord!" (*Hymns,* #240). In this way, everyone leaves singing. This is an example of sending people off.

Just as there are ten steps for singing, there are also ten steps for prayer. Ideally, one hymn should be accompanied by one or two prayers. For example, after the first hymn, a prayer should follow. After the second hymn, one or two prayers should follow. After a strengthening hymn, one or two prayers should be added. If a spirit-stirring hymn is called, it should be accompanied by a prayer that uplifts the spirit; in this way, everyone's spirit will be uplifted. In this case, there will be no need for turning, correcting, or maintaining the spirit. If there is still time, we can have more prayer and sing another hymn. This would be wonderful!

COMING TO THE MEETING
TO FUNCTION IN THE MEETING

If we meet in this way, the brothers and sisters will enjoy coming to the meetings, because they will be inwardly touched by God and will testify that God is indeed among us in our meetings. However, if we do not know how to meet when we come together, when the Holy Spirit touches a brother, he will not move. Then the Holy Spirit will find another brother, who will also ignore Him. The Holy Spirit will then come to yet another brother, who also may not think that the meeting is his responsibility. Thus, the Holy Spirit will not be able to find a channel, and the meeting will be poor. As a result, some may then even take the opportunity to speak many strange things.

For example, a brother may begin with praises and thanksgiving, but because no one follows, another will stand up and speak something strange. If no one is willing to stop the strange speaking, he will continue; however, if the saints had followed the spirit to pray, the strange speaking would never have been released. If the brothers and sisters are not willing to bear the responsibility and no one is willing to pray, all kinds of strange speaking will find a way to come out in the meeting. We should not blame those who speak strange things. Rather, we should blame ourselves for not bearing the responsibility. If such a situation continues, many brothers and sisters may find it unbearable and stop coming to the meeting. Therefore, we must all bear responsibility in the meetings and allow the Holy Spirit to use us as channels. This is a great matter, for which we need to be cautious and pray much.

We must take the meetings seriously and not conduct ourselves according to our mood and excitement. We all need to realize that we come to a meeting to fulfill our priestly ministry, to function; we do not come to take care of our mood and excitement. If we start work at eight, we should be at our place of work exactly at eight. Likewise, whenever we come to the meeting, we must mean business. We need to diligently exercise our spirit. We should exercise our spirit when we are happy and when we are unhappy. We need to take the meeting as our responsibility. When we come to the meeting, we should function in the meeting and bear the burden of the meeting.

PRAYING IN THE TABLE MEETING

There are a few points that require our attention regarding our prayer in the Lord's table meeting. First, our prayer must be related to the preceding hymn. Second, our prayer must go further and higher. It should not be lower or even parallel to the preceding one. Third, we must pay attention to the feeling of the meeting and press forward with the spirit of the meeting. Fourth, we should use utterances with poetic qualities; do not be dull or crude. Fifth, our prayer should bring the meeting to its subject. Sixth, we should avoid ritualistic formalities and instead seek to use words of revelation. When we pray in the table meeting, we must firmly grasp these six points.

CHAPTER FOUR

SELECTING HYMNS
IN THE FELLOWSHIP MEETING
AND THE LORD'S TABLE MEETING

TEN KINDS OF HYMNS IN THE COURSE OF A MEETING

In the course of a meeting, there is the need for ten different kinds of hymns: first, for opening; second, for introducing the subject; third, for strengthening; fourth, for uplifting the spirit; fifth, for turning; sixth, for correction; seventh, for maintaining the spirit; eighth, for filling up the time; ninth, for conclusion; and tenth, for lingering or sending off. Also, if we do not know the categories of hymns, the nature of the hymns, it will be difficult for us to consider other matters. In order to select hymns in a meeting, we must first know the nature of the hymns; some hymns are on gospel preaching, some are on spiritual warfare, others are on praising, and yet others are on building. We must know the different hymn categories before we can properly select them. The progression of the Lord's table meeting and the prayer meeting can be divided into ten steps or sections. A meeting does not always require this many sections, but in general it may consist of not more than these ten sections.

At the beginning of a meeting, we should select an opening hymn with much consideration. After the opening hymn we need an introductory hymn to lead us to the subject of the meeting. If the spirit of the meeting is not strong enough after the introduction, we need to call a strengthening hymn. However, if the spirit is still not strong enough, we should select a hymn that uplifts the spirit. Sometimes the introductory hymn may lead to the wrong subject. For example, if we should be praising, but someone selects a hymn concerning confessing our sins, there is the need for an immediate turn, or a correction. For example, in a Lord's table meeting someone may choose a hymn for the worship of the Father while we are still remembering the Lord, or in a prayer meeting someone may choose a hymn of praise. In both of these instances there is the need for turning. During a meeting that is prolonged, there may be the need for a hymn to maintain the spirit, to prevent the spirit from being weakened. In order to fill up the time, there also may be the need for a time-filling hymn. Finally, there is a concluding hymn. However, there are times after a meeting has ended when everyone wants to linger on. When this happens, we can choose a hymn to send everyone off. I hope we can remember all of these principles in selecting hymns.

AN EXERCISE IN SELECTING HYMNS
FOR THE FELLOWSHIP MEETING

Selecting the Opening Hymn

Now let us consider the hymns for the fellowship meeting. Suppose the saints are like plain water that is neither sweet nor sour nor spicy and thus are indifferent toward the Lord when they come together for the fellowship meeting. Which hymn should we select for opening the meeting? Someone may suggest *Hymns,* #395, "O Jesus Christ, grow Thou in me, / And all thing else recede." This hymn is not appropriate. It is not a general hymn but rather has a specific purpose; such a hymn can be used in leading to a particular subject. Another person may suggest *Hymns,* #960, "My King will soon come back again." This hymn is acceptable but still not adequate. Because it is a longer hymn, it is suitable as an opening hymn, to give the saints time for their hearts to be settled and for their spirits to be uplifted. This hymn is a better choice than *Hymns,* #395 because it reminds us of the condition at the Lord's coming back.

Hymns, #423, "Thou hidden love of God," is also good because it does not have a specific theme. Hymn #352 in the Chinese hymnal, "Though we waver as the seasons, / He will every change endure," is a good hymn and is probably the best choice for a fellowship meeting, but we cannot sing this hymn every time. Consequently, we need to have more hymns in reserve. We need to practice continually. *Hymns,* #578, "My will is weak, my strength is frail," is quite a deep hymn. Hymn #625 in the Chinese hymnal, "O Lord, we gather before Thy face," has the flavor of spiritual pursuit and may therefore be used in a prayer meeting. Hymn #353 in the Chinese hymnal, "Once I had a fervent heart," is somewhat related to spiritual pursuit and may also be used in a prayer meeting.

Hymns, #693, "He faileth not, for He is God," is not that suitable because the train of thought in this hymn does not match our subject. *Hymns,* #437, "Hast thou heard Him, seen Him, known Him," is also inappropriate because the feeling of this hymn is very high. In the fellowship meeting, which does not have a particular subject, we should not use hymns that have a specific subject. *Hymns,* #720, "God hath not promised skies always blue, / Flower-strewn pathways all our lives through," is not suitable. This is a good hymn to sing to comfort those who have suffered a domestic misfortune. *Hymns,* #370, "Abide with me! fast falls the eventide," is not suitable. If we sing this hymn to enjoy the Lord's presence when the sun is setting, it would be quite good. Or if someone is dying, we can sing this hymn with his or her family.

Hymns, #492, "In all thy work, O Lord, Thou didst," is a very deep hymn with a specific subject; hence, it is not suitable as an opening hymn. *Hymns,* #207, "Lord Jesus! when we think of Thee, / Of all Thy love and grace," is toward the Lord; hence, it cannot be used as an opening hymn in a fellowship meeting. *Hymns,* #333, "I know not why God's wondrous grace / To me He hath made known," cannot be used because the chorus is a quotation from the Bible; it is very specific. *Hymns,* #707 is on counting God's blessing and therefore is not appropriate. *Hymns,* #657, "Can you be obedient / To the Lord of all," is a challenging hymn and therefore is not suitable. *Hymns,* #1048, "Just as I am, without one plea," should be used in gospel preaching. *Hymns,* #397, "More holiness give me," can be sung at the beginning of a fellowship meeting when there is a feeling of insipidness. *Hymns,* #280, "Lord, may Thy blood now cleanse me, / Wash all my sins away," is barely acceptable. *Hymns,* #705, "In some way or other the Lord will provide," is very specific and therefore not appropriate.

The Principle in Selecting Hymns

Hymns are for the expression of feelings. We cannot sing a hymn that expresses a certain feeling if we do not have one. We should find a hymn that best expresses our feeling. Hence, we must learn how to select hymns. This means that when we touch a certain atmosphere, according to the prevailing feeling in the meeting, we should select a hymn from the hymnal that expresses that feeling best. When we choose a hymn in this way, the feeling will be expressed and will flow out through the singing of the congregation. This is the principle of selecting hymns.

Sensing the Feeling of Those Who Are Singing

When selecting a hymn, we need to sense the feeling of the saints when they are singing. Suppose there is a general feeling of insipidness in a meeting; if a hymn is selected that is very solemn, no one will be able to follow. Someone may select *Hymns,* #240, "Glory, honor, praise and power, / Be unto the Lamb forever!" In such a meeting, no one will be able to sing with any feeling of "glory" or "honor." In the same way, it would not be appropriate for us to select a hymn asking the Lord to reveal Himself if there is a need for a hymn on the confession of sins. When people are sad, we should choose hymns of sorrow; when people are joyful, we should choose hymns of rejoicing.

Selecting Hymns to Strengthen the Meeting

It is not easy to select hymns. Often our meetings are not strong because our feeling is not keen. Some brothers have fellowshipped that the meetings in their localities are not strong. I would ask, "If our feeling is not keen, how can the meetings be strong?" According to our observation, we sense that the meetings are not satisfactory. Hence, we urgently need to be trained in these three matters: first, how to work; second, how to lead; and third, how to manage.

Leading the meetings is not the responsibility of the elders and deacons only; it is the responsibility of all the saints. Hence, we have an obligation to learn to select hymns. If we are unable to select appropriate hymns, how can we have good meetings? Although there may be no particular feeling at the beginning of a fellowship meeting, the principle for selecting hymns still applies. Consider hymn #128 in the Chinese hymnal, "I prostrate, Lord, before Thee, / Marvel at boundless grace." This hymn expresses the feeling of a person who has been touched by the Lord's love and feels that he is loved by the Lord. By singing this hymn of love, he is able to express all of his feelings. However, because this is a specific hymn, it should not be called at the beginning of a fellowship meeting, a meeting without a particular feeling. The principle of choosing hymns is that we should choose a hymn according to the feeling we sense in the meeting.

In a general fellowship meeting, it is good to select hymn #352 in the Chinese hymnal, "Though we waver as the seasons, / He will every change endure." Our inspiration to select this hymn indicates that we feel the Lord is dear to us. As we sing this hymn, a feeling for the Lord replaces our indifference. This is very good. After singing, we should follow with a prayer. We may pray, "O Lord, we were so indifferent when we came before You, yet Your love toward us has never changed. Thank You, Lord." Once we sing this hymn and pray in this way, the hearts of the brothers and sisters will be brought to a state where they have a feeling for the Lord. The meeting will then have a center, a subject, which is the Lord's dearness to us and His love for us to the uttermost. Then we can lead the meeting to this subject.

Selecting an Introductory Hymn

Let us consider selecting an introductory hymn. Even though *Hymns,* #544, "Lord Jesus, I love Thee, I know Thou art mine," is a good hymn, after singing it we will not be left with a strong feeling because this hymn does not touch the Lord's love but touches our lack of love for the Lord. *Hymns,* #368, "More love to Thee, O Lord," is the same. However, *Hymns,* #286, "Of Jesus' love that sought me," is very good as a continuation of the opening hymn, hymn #352 in the Chinese hymnal. *Hymns,* #286 speaks of Jesus' love that is "far deeper than the sea"; the chorus also speaks of Jesus' love. Thus, it conveniently leads us to the subject. *Hymns,* #956, "Soon our Lord will come, the day is drawing nigh," causes us to consider the Lord Jesus' coming and therefore is not appropriate for leading the meeting to the subject of the Lord's love.

We have said repeatedly that selecting hymns is a matter of feeling; hence, we need to touch the feeling of the spirit. If we are indifferent when we come together for a fellowship meeting, there is a need for someone to touch a particular feeling. If this feeling is touched, we will be able to choose the most suitable hymn. For instance, we may select hymn #352 in the Chinese hymnal. The more we sing this hymn, the more we will feel that even though we are cold toward the Lord, He is never cold toward us; that even though our heart may often change, His love will never depart; and that even though we do not care for the Lord, He cares very much for us. After we sing this hymn with such feeling, we should immediately follow with a prayer, thanking the Lord for His unchanging love. In this way, our hearts will be stirred up to follow the Lord.

The Lord has never changed toward us. Although we may feel indifferent when we came into the meeting, through singing and prayer and the introductory hymn, *Hymns,* #286, the feeling of the Lord's love being far deeper than the sea will be stirred up within us, and we will be led to the subject.

Understanding the Purpose of Hymns

In order to select hymns, we must first know the purpose of hymns. Why do we need to sing hymns in a meeting? The hymns that the brothers and sisters typically select show that we do not know the purpose of selecting hymns, and we do not know that a hymn is a poem. A poem is for the expression of feelings. The Chinese say that a poem is an inspiration. A poem is different than an essay. Whereas an essay may be written according to a train of thought, a poem requires inspiration. To be inspired is to be aroused with a feeling. We must be touched before we can write a poem. Without any feeling, there will be no poem. A poem, a hymn, is the expression of our feeling. When we come together to choose hymns, we must hold firmly to this secret.

There is always an atmosphere when the saints gather together. We need to learn to sense the atmosphere, the feeling. When we touch the atmosphere, the feeling, we can select an appropriate hymn from our memory that matches the feeling we sense. At the end of a meeting, if we sense that the feeling of the brothers and sisters is that the Lord Jesus is exalted, we should sing "All in all forever, / Only Christ I'll sing" (*Hymns,* #513, chorus). This hymn can express the feeling of the brothers' and sisters' exaltation of Christ.

Since a hymn is for the expression of feelings, we must touch the feeling of the ones who are singing when we select a hymn. If a hymn matches the feeling of those who are singing, they will be released and will express their inner feeling through the hymn. Hence, we must be familiar with the hymns. We must ask, "What is the feeling of this particular hymn? Is the feeling adequately conveyed?" We need to be familiar with these points; then when we touch a certain feeling in a meeting, we will be able to select a hymn from our memory. Then everyone's feeling will be expressed through the singing.

A PRACTICAL EXERCISE IN SELECTING HYMNS IN THE LORD'S TABLE MEETING

Selecting an Opening Hymn

One time there were many attendants in a Lord's table meeting, but the atmosphere of the meeting was plain and somewhat indifferent. Someone selected hymn #128 in the Chinese hymnal, "I prostrate, Lord, before Thee, / Marvel at boundless grace," and a brother changed it to *Hymns,* #213, "On that same night, Lord Jesus, / When all around Thee joined." This was a good change. First, this showed that the brother knew how to change hymns; second, it showed that he knew how to touch the atmosphere. After singing *Hymns,* #213, there were three to four prayers that failed to match this hymn. In fact, the prayers neither touched nor came up to the level of the atmosphere. We should not ignore the atmosphere in a meeting, paying attention merely to our feeling and praying formal, conventional prayers. As a rule, after singing *Hymns,* #213 a brother should offer a prayer based on the feeling of the hymn to bring the atmosphere of the meeting forward. In brief, this hymn says, "Lord Jesus, at Your last supper on earth, all around You was a dark shadow, and the situation was so difficult, but You still established Your supper for us to remember You. Apparently, it is we who remember You; actually, it is You who remember us. How could we be saved on that long, long night if You had not chosen and called us? Even today we are here remembering You because of Your grace." In our prayer, we need to bring the saints' feeling deeper into the Lord, in order for them to sense that we remember the Lord because He first remembered us. When we offer such a prayer, the feeling of the saints will be turned to the Lord.

Introducing and Strengthening the Subject of the Lord's Table Meeting

Let us consider how to introduce the subject of the Lord's table meeting. *Hymns,* #87, which says, "O Lord! When we the path retrace / Which Thou on earth has trod," is neither good nor bad. However, *Hymns,* #158 is very good. This hymn speaks of how the Lord sought and found us and how He gave Himself for us. It is a very fitting hymn to continue the feeling of the previous hymn. After singing *Hymns,* #213 it would be good if someone had prayed, "O Lord, we thank and praise You. Before You departed from us, You established this table for us to remember You. We see that this bread is the body You gave for us, and this cup is the blood of the covenant, the blood You shed for us. We cannot but thank and worship You. Lord, You gave Your body and shed Your blood for us as the portion You have given us. Today we come especially to remember You and express our love for You."

How should we select a second hymn? Someone may suggest *Hymns,* #437, "Hast thou heard Him, seen Him, known Him," but this is not suitable. We must firmly grasp this principle: we need to touch the feeling of the meeting. After singing *Hymns,* #213 and offering a prayer on how the Lord gave Himself and shed His blood for us, we could also continue with *Hymns,* #65, "Jesus! that name we love." Stanza 2 is especially appropriate, saying, "As Son of Man it was, / Jesus, the Lord! / Thou gav'st Thy life for us, / Jesus, our Lord! / Great was indeed Thy love, / All other loves above, / Love Thou didst dearly prove, / Jesus, our Lord!" This hymn continues the feeling of the earlier prayer and further strengthens the subject.

THE LORD'S TABLE MEETING BEING FOR THE REMEMBRANCE OF THE LORD'S PERSON, LIVING, SUFFERING, DEATH, EXALTATION, AND GLORIFICATION

In order to remember the Lord in the Lord's table meeting, we need to see that it is the Lord's person and work that are worthy of our remembrance. First, we need to see the person of the Lord, to see who He is. We must see the two aspects of His person: He is God yet man; He is the Creator yet a creature. To remember the Lord is to come into the presence of the Lord and worship Him.

Second, we need to see the Lord's living on earth. This includes His humbling Himself, His humiliation, and His human virtues. Hence, at the Lord's table, we first need to see the Lord's person and then His human living. Regarding the Lord's human living, *Hymns,* #87 says that the Lord showed His faithfulness to God and His wondrous love and grace to men.

Third, we need to remember the Lord's suffering and death. There are many hymns on the Lord's death, such as *Hymns,* #101, #104, and #95. We may also say that this is to remember the Lord's work in redemption.

Fourth, we need to remember the Lord's exaltation, including His ascension and glorification. Our remembrance of the Lord consists basically around these four major points: His person, His living, His suffering and death, and His ascension and glorification. We remember the Lord for the things that transpired in the past, and we look forward to His coming back, which is something in the future. There are other items that are included in these major points; for example, the Lord's name is included in His exaltation, and His being the eternal Savior is included in His person. Furthermore, there are many small items, such as the Lord's humility, the Lord's washing His disciples' feet, and the Lord's appearing to Mary. Nonetheless, there are four major points: first, the Lord's person; second, the Lord's human living, including all of His situations; third, the Lord's death; and fourth, the Lord's exaltation.

Which item should we remember when we gather around the Lord's table? Should we remember the Lord's person, His living, His death, or His exaltation? How can we discern? If we sing *Hymns,* #213, followed by *Hymns,* #158 to bring in a subject, we are remembering the third item of the Lord—the Lord's death in His work. The Lord's death, however, did not begin with His crucifixion. His death began with His birth in the manger in Bethlehem. It would be very good to sing *Hymns,* #158 to remember the Lord's death in His redemptive work. If after singing *Hymns,* #158 the meeting is strong and does not need further strengthening, and the spirit is high and does not need further uplifting, what should we do? One of the brothers may add a prayer.

What should we do after a strong prayer has been offered and there is a need to maintain the spirit? We may bless the bread and the cup. Brothers and sisters, we must pay attention to this: when the spirit of the meeting is at its highest point, when the meeting has reached a climax, there is no need to choose a hymn or add a prayer for strengthening. Instead, there should be brothers who take the lead to bless the bread and the cup. There are no regulations in our meeting regarding how many hymns should be sung and how many prayers should be offered before we bless the bread and the cup. One time in a Lord's table meeting, everyone sang over and over, they prayed, knelt down and stood up, and prayed and sang again for at least fifty minutes, but no one would bless the bread and the cup. This can be compared to country people who invite others to a meal at twelve noon but still have not served them by three o'clock in the afternoon. We need to take care of the atmosphere and feeling of the meeting. I hope that the churches in different places will instruct the saints regarding these points.

We need to be watchful in spirit in the table meeting. We must bless the bread and the cup when the meeting reaches a climax and cannot go any higher. After we bless the bread and the cup and pass them around, there is a need to maintain the spirit with a hymn. We may use *Hymns,* #136, "Gazing on the Lord in glory, / While our hearts in worship bow," or *Hymns,* #226, "For the bread and for the wine, / For the pledge that seals Him mine." In contrast, *Hymns,* #226 bears a flavor of ritualistic formalities. We must touch the feeling of the meeting. In order to not allow the spirit to be weakened when we pass the bread and cup, we need to select a hymn that can maintain the spirit. At this point the selection of a hymn greatly depends on the prayers offered during the blessing of the bread and the cup. After singing *Hymns,* #158, someone may bless the bread and the cup, praying, "O Lord, thank You for first remembering us. You shed Your blood and died for us in this wilderness. The bread and the cup show us the story of Your giving up Your life and shedding Your blood for us. The scene of Your crucifixion is before our eyes. You wore a crown of thorns, and Your head was full of bruises. Lord, we thank You." Someone else may continue and pray, "Lord, the picture of Your coming down to the earth from heaven to shed Your blood and die for us is vividly before us." In such a case it would be good if someone selected *Hymns,* #95, "O Head once full of bruises, / So full of pain and scorn." The hymn selected should be according to the prayer that blessed the bread and the cup.

Hymns, #93, "Lord, we treasure with affection / All Thy path of sorrow here," is also good. This hymn is better than *Hymns,* #95 in continuing *Hymns,* #158. The fourth stanza of *Hymns,* #93 is the highest, speaking of sin's distance and how far-reaching it is: "Thou didst measure then sin's distance, / Darkness, wrath and curse were Thine; / Man-betrayed, by God forsaken; / Thus we learn Thy love divine!" The contents of this stanza show the far-reaching scope of sin. Even though the Lord went through all these sufferings, we do not know the far-reaching scope of sin. Nevertheless, the Lord experienced all these things personally, measuring out the distance of sin, enabling us to see the length of sin's distance: darkness, wrath, and the curse. It is not until we have such a realization that we can know the loveliness of the Lord. If we want to touch the feeling of a meeting, we must at least understand the meaning expressed through the words of the hymns.

CHAPTER FIVE

SELECTING HYMNS AND PRAYING IN THE LORD'S TABLE MEETING AND THE PRAYER MEETING

Let us consider further how to select hymns in the meetings. At the climax of the Lord's table meeting, in order to maintain the spirit of the meeting after the bread and the cup have been blessed and passed, there is the need to fill up the rest of the time with hymns and prayers. Then the meeting should turn to the second section, which is the worship of the Father.

TURNING THE ATMOSPHERE OF THE MEETING FROM PRAISING THE LORD TO WORSHIPPING THE FATHER

When we worship the Father, we do not need a new beginning; we simply need to make a turn. A hymn for praising the Father is also a hymn for worshipping the Father. Although the worship of the Father is another section, it still needs to be linked to the previous section. For example, in the first section of the table meeting if we have seen the Lord's redemptive love that seeks and brings us back, we should turn to the worship of the Father with this feeling. In such a feeling we can worship God the Father for sending the Lord Jesus to the earth. Hence, our praising and singing will provide a flavor of the Father's sending of the Son. However, if we select *Hymns,* #178, "Our hearts are full of Christ and long / Their glorious matter to declare," we will certainly go backward. This is not acceptable. Instead, *Hymns,* #42 would be a good choice, "By Thee, O God, invited, / We look unto the Son, / In whom Thy heart delighted, / Who all Thy will hath done; / And by the one chief treasure / Thy bosom freely gave, / Thine own pure love we measure, / Thy willing mind to save," because it meets the requirement of worshipping the Father, and its taste is also higher.

When we worship the Father, we often call *Hymns,* #33 or *Hymns,* #52, without paying attention to the theme of our remembrance of the Lord. Hence, our spirit often cannot follow when it is time to worship the Father. This is because we do not enter into the atmosphere and feeling of the meeting; we do not enter into the spirit of the hymns that were selected in the section on remembering the Lord.

BRINGING THE WORSHIP OF THE FATHER TO A CLIMAX AND SENDING PEOPLE OFF

If we have seen the Lord's redemptive love, when we turn to worship the Father, the feeling of such worship should be based upon the Father's sending His beloved Son to redeem us. Thus, we should select a second hymn. If we select *Hymns,* #52, however, it may be too quick. We can also turn from the feeling of the Lord's coming to seek us to the praise of the Father's love, matching this with prayers that praise the Father's love and then proceed forward. Even though *Hymns,* #299, "A mind at perfect peace with God," is not a hymn on the worship of the Father, it can be used. After singing this hymn, it would be good if someone were to stand up and pray, "O Father, thank You for sending the Lord Jesus to seek us. In Your love we were sought and brought back. Now before You in Your house, we enjoy the love You prepared for us in eternity." After such a prayer, we can call *Hymns,* #43, "'Abba, Father,' we adore Thee, / While the hosts in heaven above / E'en in us now learn the wonders / Of Thy wisdom, grace, and love. / Soon before Thy throne assembled, / All Thy children shall proclaim / Abba's love shown in redemption, / And how full is Abba's name!" Singing this hymn can be compared to putting on a vest in fall; we feel just right, neither cold nor hot.

It is good for a brother to choose *Hymns,* #45, but we should avoid singing two hymns of a similar nature in succession. It would be too much for us to sing *Hymns,* #45 after singing *Hymns,* #43. After the singing, either a brother or a sister can offer a prayer, saying, "Our God, because You have chosen us before the creation of the world, now in Your love we have come back to Your house." This is another turn, from the praise of the Father's love to the praise of the Father's choosing. After the praises, we can call *Hymns,* #33, "Father, long before creation, / Thou hadst chosen us in love; / And that love, so deep, so moving, / Draws us close to Christ above, / And will keep us, and will keep us, / Firmly fixed in Christ alone..." This is truly good and can be compared to singing hymns of ascent, going up higher and higher, step by step, waiting for the bread and the cup to be put back on the table. Then at the end of the hymn, that is, at the climax of the worship of the Father, a brother should lead everyone to stand up and conclude the meeting with a prayer.

However, sometimes even though the meeting has ended, everyone may still be unwilling to depart and want to continue. At this time there is the need for sending off by singing the last stanza of *Hymns,* #33 again. I hope that we could all see that this is a lesson we should learn and practice. In this way, we will be able to function in the meetings.

PRAYERS IN THE TABLE MEETING

Like the singing of hymns, the prayer in the table meeting has different sections. There are opening prayers, introductory prayers, strengthening prayers, spirit-uplifting prayers, spirit-maintaining prayers, turning prayers, correcting prayers, time-filling prayers, concluding prayers, and sending-off prayers. Just as singing has its steps, prayer also has its process with many sections. I hope that we will remember this principle and will practice it diligently so that we may function in the meeting, like an experienced basketball team.

If the feeling of the saints is plain and indifferent at the Lord's table, we can select *Hymns,* #213, "On that same night, Lord Jesus, / When all around Thee joined / To cast its darkest shadow / Across Thy holy mind." After singing this hymn, the saints should have some feeling. When we touch this feeling, we should immediately offer a prayer. If we sense that the prayer is vague, we can share our feeling with the saints.

There are a few points that we must grasp firmly and take heed to. First, we must come out of our own feeling when we pray in the meeting. Second, we must be able to follow and touch the feeling and the atmosphere we sense when in the meeting. Whether it is our selecting of hymns, testifying, or praying, it must follow the flow of the Holy Spirit. Sadly, very few brothers and sisters pray this kind of prayer in the meeting. Almost all the brothers and sisters bring their personal feelings into their prayers in the meeting.

For example, after singing a hymn of praise to the Lord for His glory and greatness, a sister may pray in tears, "O Lord, I am really suffering, but I thank and praise You for the cross You have given me." She was not moved to tears while praying; rather, she had tears in her eyes when she was on her way to the meeting. Immediately after singing the hymn, her prayer with tears quickly brings her own feeling into the meeting, completely ignoring the feeling and atmosphere of the meeting. All sorts of strange thoughts can be brought into the meeting. Therefore, we should not hold on to our personal feeling. As soon as we enter a meeting, we should sense and closely follow the atmosphere of the meeting.

Third, we should try our best to avoid ritualistic formalities in our prayers. For example, in a table meeting we may sing *Hymns,* #226, "For the bread and for the wine, / For the pledge that seals Him mine." At the last stanza, when we are uplifted in our spirit, a brother may take the lead to stand up to bless the bread and the cup. However, another brother may stand up and pray, "Lord, we thank You for gathering us here to remember You. Lord, we praise You for calming our hearts, causing our hearts not to be disturbed or distracted." If the ritualistic phrases were removed from his prayer, there would be nothing left. This may be compared to writing a letter full of ritualistic expressions; eventually, no one will understand the letter. Prayers that contain many ritualistic expressions sound insincere. We should do our best to avoid using ritualistic phrases; rather, we should pray with clear utterances concerning the Lord's bread and cup: "Lord, this is Your bread and cup, which we receive from Your hand. Grant us the realization that it is because Your body was broken for us that we may have Your life, and that it is because Your precious blood was shed for us that we can be filled with Your comfort." This kind of prayer is clear and accurate; it is uttered with powerful words and void of superfluous ritualistic phrases.

Many of our prayers in the meeting contain too many ceremonial expressions and very few words of revelation. We must learn to follow our inner feeling at all times. In order to express our spiritual feeling, we need to practice. We are often short of the utterance for these feelings. This is because we lack practice. Hence, we need to practice in order to have eloquence for our spiritual utterance at all times.

Furthermore, when we comment on the prayers of the brothers and sisters, we must never criticize. Criticism comes out of the flesh and is the issue of partaking of the tree of the knowledge of good and evil, which opens people's eyes. We need to learn to have a kind of spiritual study that enables us to make progress in spiritual matters.

For example, a brother may pray too quickly in a table meeting, not in terms of his words but in terms of his proceeding directly to bless the bread and the cup at the beginning of the meeting. It is too quick to mention the bread and the cup in the first prayer in the meeting. Even though his prayer is strong in words and in spirit, the quality of his prayer is low. We must hold firmly to the principle that after the first hymn in a table meeting, the first prayer should not be too quick to mention the bread and the cup. Our prayer should be the same as our singing, it should be of high quality.

If we can pray, "Lord, we are here to remember You because in the evening when You departed from us, You left us with a charge to remember You. Today we are here, seemingly remembering You, but in fact, it is You who first remembers us. You have remembered us from eternity. There has never been a moment in time that You are not thinking of us. This is the reason we can be here to remember You today." Such a prayer proceeds higher and higher without mentioning the bread and the cup. It reaches the point where we sense that the Lord is remembering us, and in this remembrance we have fellowship with Him. On the one hand, we worship Him, and on the other hand, we contemplate Him. This kind of prayer is high in quality.

First Samuel 2 in the Old Testament records the praise of Samuel's mother when she offered Samuel to God (vv. 1-10). The quality of her praise was high. In the New Testament, Mary, the mother of the Lord Jesus, in the flesh, also offered praise that was high in quality (Luke 1:46-55). Another example is Paul's prayer in Ephesians 1, which says, "That the God of our Lord Jesus Christ, the Father of glory, may give to you a spirit of wisdom and revelation in the full knowledge of Him" (v. 17). This prayer is high. Then in chapter 3, the prayer and praise are even higher (vv. 16-21). Hence, we need to practice so that our prayer, praise, and hymns can be uplifted.

SELECTING HYMNS IN THE PRAYER MEETING

Now let us consider how to select hymns in the prayer meeting. Suppose in the meeting we sense that the atmosphere is depressed, the enemy's attack is there, and the spirit of the saints is very heavy; perhaps the church has some problems, or some brothers and sisters are ill or have suffered some hardships in their homes. How should we select a hymn in this situation?

Like the table meeting, the prayer meeting has different sections. The table meeting has ten sections, but the prayer meeting may be for spiritual warfare, for spiritual pursuit, for the gospel work, for the revival of the church, for specific matters, or for general affairs. When the atmosphere of the meeting is depressed, we need prayers of spiritual warfare. Although the Lord's table meeting and the prayer meeting are different in their nature, content, and items, their course is the same. In selecting a hymn, we always have to hold on to the principle that the meaning of the words in the hymn must match the feeling we sense in the meeting.

After singing, we should pray one after another. Sometimes, when the allotted time for a prayer meeting is long, we need to use a hymn to fill the time, stir up the saints, and maintain the spirit. We can sing *Hymns,* #890, "Hallelujah! Christ is Victor." However, it is better not to sing the whole hymn;

rather, it is sufficient to sing only one stanza and the chorus. We can also sing *Hymns,* #880; this hymn strengthens the brothers and sisters in their inner feeling to oppose Satan. After the prayer, when the spirit has been released to the point that our utterance has been exhausted, we may express this feeling through a hymn. When everyone is released in the singing, a brother needs to add a prayer. At this time it may seem that the meeting is over. But if the meeting has a lingering taste, and there is a need to send people off, we can sing the chorus of *Hymns,* #890 again. This can be compared to wrapping a gift perfectly and then adding a beautiful bow. If the saints attend this kind of meeting, they will surely like to continue meeting.

Our problem is that we always seem to have a good beginning but not a good ending. This is because we are not familiar with the hymns. Thus, we not only need to know the principle of selecting hymns, we also need to study and practice selecting hymns. From now on the responsible brothers should practice selecting hymns in all the fellowship meetings of the church. Then our meetings will spontaneously be good and rich.

Moreover, there is a great principle with regard to singing. It is acceptable to sing slowly when we are alone, but if we sing slowly in a big meeting, the whole meeting will be finished. It is good to sing slowly in private, but we should not bring the same slowness into the meetings. Furthermore, I hope that all the brothers in various localities who can sing would not rely on only one or two to lead the singing. In a meeting all those who know how to sing should lead the singing, and those who do not know how to sing should not begin a tune. In other words, all those who do not have the confidence should not lead the singing, but those who can sing should not wait for others to lead the singing. Everyone must function properly.

CHAPTER SIX

A PRACTICAL EXERCISE OF PRAYING IN THE LORD'S TABLE MEETING

(1)

If we consider these exercises for the meetings as something too difficult and not worthwhile, there is nothing further to say. But if we think that these exercises are worthwhile, we should apply ourselves, spend our time, and learn to put ourselves aside particularly in this matter. Otherwise, these exercises will only be in letter; there will not be much spiritual significance. If we are not willing to pay the price, what we are doing can be compared to building a castle in the air. Therefore, if we are willing to pay the price, we must diligently apply ourselves to be exercised in this matter. This kind of exercise will yield no result if we do not have the heart for it.

Moreover, if we want good and rich meetings, we must allow the Holy Spirit to rule. The Holy Spirit cannot come out in a meeting unless He can first come out through us. Therefore, we must allow Him to reign in us by simply laying ourselves aside.

PRAYER IN THE LORD'S TABLE MEETING

Usually, at the beginning of the table meeting everyone feels quite ordinary; we do not have any particular feeling. In such a case we can select *Hymns,* #158, "Lord, Thy love has sought and found us / Wand'ring in this desert wide; / Thou hast thrown Thine arms around us, / For us suffered, bled, and died. / Sing, my soul! He lovèd thee, / Jesus gave Himself for me." This hymn can easily touch the feeling deep within us. On the one hand, it gives us a sense of the Lord's coming to seek us and His giving Himself up for us; on the other hand, it stirs up a sense of gratitude in our hearts and a desire to offer up our praise to the Lord. If we are touched in our spirit after singing and have entered into the feeling of the Lord's seeking us and giving Himself up for us, a brother should offer a prayer according to this feeling in his spirit.

THE PRINCIPLE OF PRAYING
IN A LORD'S TABLE MEETING

Fitly Connected to One Another

We must pay attention to a few principles when we pray at a table meeting. First, our prayers must be fitly connected to one another. After singing a hymn that was selected according to the spirit of the meeting, we should utter a prayer to follow the hymn; we should not pray in a disconnected way. We should sense the feeling of a meeting by following the Spirit's moving within us. In a meeting we should be like those in a relay race in which we may not run outside the lane. After singing the first hymn, someone should follow with a prayer. After the first prayer, someone else should follow with a second hymn or a second prayer, and perhaps there should be a third prayer. The entire meeting, including the selection of hymns, prayers, reading of Scriptures, exhortation, or testimony, should be carried out as if we are in a relay race; there should not be another beginning halfway through the meeting.

The present situation in our meetings is that we have one beginning after another, with each person making his own move. Five people have five different activities; ten people have ten different activities. From the beginning to the end, our meetings are continually being restarted. Thus, the entire meeting is disconnected, without a distinct beginning, progression, or conclusion. This is a serious mistake. We must firmly grasp this principle: with the exception of the beginning prayer, all subsequent prayers, whether it is one prayer or ten prayers, must be connected with each other and closely follow each other.

Moving Forward in the Spirit

Second, our prayers should move forward; they should not remain in the same place. Immediately after we offer a prayer in relation to a hymn, we must move forward in our spirit. We must not only move further but also move higher. For instance, when we follow *Hymns,* #158 with a prayer, our spirit must not remain in the same place; it should move forward. Horizontally, our prayer should advance further; vertically, it should climb higher. The first prayer leads to the subject; hence, the second prayer should climb one step higher, and then when another hymn is selected, it should climb even higher. We must hold on to this principle. Just as in writing a composition, we keep moving higher and further.

Maintaining the Feeling of the Meeting

Third, as we move forward in the meeting, we must learn to maintain the feeling of the meeting in our prayers and hymns. This simply means that we cannot proceed independently. As we move forward in selecting a hymn, and especially when we pray, we should bring the brothers and sisters with us. The more we pray, the more they will say Amen; the more we pray, the more they will be drawn to the center. The brothers and sisters may not be uplifted in their spirit before we pray, but after we pray, their spirits should climb higher and higher.

Suppose the brothers and sisters are in the feeling of the Lord's suffering, yet our prayer is concerning the Lord's glorification in heaven. Our feeling does not match the feeling of the brothers and sisters. According to our feeling we have already climbed up to heaven, but the brothers and sisters are still prostrate on earth. This is not appropriate. We need to take care of the feeling of the brothers and sisters as we move upward. Hence, prayer requires a great deal of exercise. In a three-legged race, we must take care of our partner who is bound to us; we cannot simply run as fast as we wish. Likewise, as we move forward in a meeting, we must bring the brothers and sisters with us and run with them. Do not disregard this matter. This requires a considerable amount of exercise.

Using Utterances of Poetic Quality

Fourth, as a rule, all of our prayers should contain utterances of poetic quality. We should pray with words that bear a poetic character; it is not good to pray with words that are too plain. For example, the Canaanite woman cried out to the Lord Jesus: "Have mercy on me, Lord, Son of David!" (Matt. 15:22). Her prayer has a poetic nature as evidenced by the utterances *Have mercy on me* and *Son of David*. She came to ask the Son of David to heal her daughter. Without the poetic characteristic, she might have asked the Lord in a rough way, "Just heal my daughter." This kind of prayer is not wrong. She might have also said, "Jesus, my daughter is ill. Go quickly and heal her!" This would make her sound like a bandit who always speaks rudely to coerce people to do something, saying, "You do this!" However, although she was a Canaanite woman, when she came to pray before the Lord Jesus, her prayer was poetic: "Have mercy on me, Lord, Son of David! My daughter suffers terribly from demon possession" (v. 22). Her utterances are refined and pleasant to the ears. Hence, there is a great deal for us to learn regarding prayer.

The Lord Jesus was even more poetic in His reply. He was not like us; we might have said directly, "Go away; I cannot heal your daughter." The Lord did not do this; rather, He replied in a mild way, "It is not good to take the children's bread and throw it to the little dogs" (v. 26). The word *dogs* implies many things. The Canaanite woman's answer was very proper: "Yes, Lord, for even the little dogs eat of the crumbs which fall from their masters' table" (v. 27). The conversation between her and the Lord contains numerous poetic utterances. There is no direct mention of the daughter's problem, yet the purpose of the entire conversation is for the daughter. This is being poetic. The Lord's response is also very poetic. He did not say, "These Gentiles do not know God; even the children of Israel do not have such faith." Instead, He said, "Great is your faith! Be it done to you as you wish" (v. 28). The Lord's response is as poetic as the Canaanite woman's prayer.

Furthermore, Jacob's blessing of his sons (Gen. 49:1-28),

Moses' blessing of the children of Israel (Deut. 33), and the prayer of Samuel's mother (1 Sam. 2:1-10) are passages in the Old Testament that are rich in poetic qualities. These qualities are especially evident in the Psalms. For example, Psalm 51 is David's psalm of repentance. He said, "Therefore You are righteous when You speak; / You are clear when You judge... / Purge my sin with hyssop, and I will be clean; / Wash me, and I will be whiter than snow... / Create in me a clean heart, O God, / And renew a steadfast spirit within me" (vv. 4-10). On the surface, these expressions seem to be very plain, but in actuality they possess rich poetic qualities. I hope that we will all pay attention to this matter and will be exercised in it. God is full of feeling. A person with much feeling tends to be poetic in utterance, whereas a person with little feeling tends to be rough in his expressions. The more a person touches God, the richer his feeling will be, and consequently, the more poetic his utterances will be.

However, do not think that merely being poetic is good enough; the most important thing concerning prayer is that it should touch people's spirit. The more we are in the spirit, the more feeling we have; the less we are in the spirit, the less feeling we have. The outward feeling of man is shallow; the inward feeling of man is deep. The spirit of man is the deepest part of man. The more we pray by the spirit, the more feeling we will have, and consequently, our utterances will be more poetic. Moreover, the more poetic our utterances are, the more we can touch the feelings of others. If our prayer is full of poetical utterance, it is easier for us to touch the spirit and the feeling of the saints. But if we use fancy words merely for the sake of being poetic, it will be ineffective and worthless.

In our service to God, we must learn to be keen and tender in our feeling. We should not use common and rough expressions. Although our prayers are neither poems nor psalms of praise, through them we can touch the Lord who has the most feeling and who is the most exalted and glorious. Therefore, when we come before the Lord to speak to Him, our utterances should be full of poetic qualities and rich in feeling.

Bringing the Saints into the Revelation

Fifth, our prayers should not only move forward and upward, they should also bring the atmosphere of the meeting to the subject of the meeting. For example, the first section of the Lord's table meeting is for the breaking of the bread. After a few hymns and prayers, we should bring the meeting toward the bread and the cup, to the feeling of breaking the bread. However, some prayers do not turn our feeling to the Lord's table but rather draw our feeling further away from it. Suppose the atmosphere at the Lord's table is that the Lord died and shed His blood for us, yet a brother prays in tears, "O Lord, no one but You can understand the hardship we suffer on earth." We cannot say that such a prayer is wrong. However, this prayer merely takes us to a Roman execution place to see the persecution of Christians; it does not show us the Lord's table.

If our spirit is focused on the bread and the cup and a prayer is offered regarding the Lord's suffering on earth, a brother should follow the prayer and the atmosphere of the meeting to select *Hymns,* #226, "For the bread and for the wine, / For the pledge that seals Him mine, / For the words of love divine, / We give Thee thanks, O Lord." This will bring us into the feeling of the bread and the cup. When we come to the fourth stanza, we should all stand up and prepare for the breaking of the bread. After singing, someone should offer a prayer of blessing to receive the bread and the cup from the Lord's hand.

Avoiding Formalities

Sixth, we should avoid formal prayers at the table meeting; instead, we should use words of revelation and words that convey spiritual facts. For instance, at the beginning of the table meeting, a brother may pray, "O Lord, once again we come to Your table." This word is formal; it is not of revelation. After singing *Hymns,* #226 we should normally have a certain feeling or seeing concerning the bread and the cup. We should not pray with formal phrases, such as "once again we...," especially if such a prayer was offered earlier in the meeting. Suppose we were invited to a meal and have been sitting for a while at the dinner table. When the food is put on the table, we should take it and eat. It would be formal for us to say, "Once again let us come and eat."

When we pray, we should simply say, "O Lord, we thank You for the bread and for the cup; we are here in remembrance of You. O Lord, thank You for giving us the bread and the cup." The principle is that we mention the bread and the cup directly. We can also say, "O Lord, our hearts are filled with sweetness as we sing with our mouths and behold the bread and the cup with our eyes. O Lord, You are the sweetest One." This is somewhat poetic. After this we can pray with words of revelation concerning the bread: "O Lord, although we are here breaking the bread, the bread was actually broken on the cross." This word is significant because it shows that we can break the bread today because the Lord was broken at the time of His crucifixion. We should continually refer to the bread in our prayers. For instance, we may say, "Lord, we praise You that You were broken; You are no longer unbroken. Because You were broken, we can have Your life, Your very person." After we have finished praying concerning the bread, we should go on to speak concerning the cup, still using words of revelation and of a poetic nature.

Then all the saints will have the inward revelation: "O Lord, the bread is so good, and the cup is so sweet. You received the cup as a portion on our behalf. You drank the cup of wrath so that today we have the cup of blessing. It is because You shed Your blood and died for us that the cup of wrath has become the cup of blessing. In this cup, we see the precious blood You shed for us. It is because You shed Your blood that our sins were taken away from us, and God's riches have come to us. O Lord, now we receive this bread and this cup from Your hand. While we are receiving them, we pray that You would add Yourself as a blessing to us. Lord, may we touch the reality of this bread and this cup, not merely the outward bread and cup. Lord, may we break this bread and drink this cup in our daily living." We must bring the brothers and sisters into the feeling of the bread and the cup.

Through our prayer, both the bread and the cup are

unveiled to the universe. After our prayer, everyone should have seen the bread and the cup. This kind of revelation is not received instantly. Therefore, we need to spend the time and energy to exercise diligently. If in every locality there are ten saints who know how to select hymns and another ten who know how to pray, the situation of the various meetings will surely be living and full of the life supply. Thus, everyone will love to come to the meeting and live the church life.

There are fifty-two weeks in a year. If week by week, we speak the story, the beauty, and the sweetness of the bread and the cup through our prayers, what a rich church life we will have! For example, when we are remembering the Lord in a table meeting, we may see the beauty of the Lord's fine living on earth. When it is time to bless the bread and the cup, someone may bless and thank the Lord for the bread and the cup, saying, "O Lord, this bread is like the cakes of fine flour in the Old Testament. Lord, You are like the fine flour. You are fine in every aspect." Then when we break the bread the following week, we may see the suffering of the Lord; thus, we bless the bread and the cup by saying, "O Lord, from the time You came to the earth, You suffered continually. Lord, You are the one grain who passed through smiting and grinding. You suffered Your whole life. Lord, the cup displayed here portrays You as a grape that was crushed, squeezed, and pressed. You have suffered so much for us. Lord, we thank You." In this way, the saints will know the Lord in His different aspects.

We must all be desperate before the Lord to avoid formal words and, instead, use words of revelation. For example, after the bread and the cup are blessed, a brother may select *Hymns,* #93. As a rule, someone should offer a prayer that follows the feeling of the hymn, saying, "O Lord, because You were betrayed by man and forsaken by God, You measured sin's distance on the cross for us. This distance includes darkness, wrath, and the curse. Here, despite such a distance, we are receiving the bread and the cup." We should then thank and praise the Lord for His cross. After this, a brother who has seen the revelation that resurrection comes after the cross should pray, "O Lord, You not only died, but You also resurrected for us. On one hand, we have seen Your death; on the other hand, we are in Your resurrection. Lord, we are here remembering You in Your resurrection. We praise You that You resurrected and that You are with us now and forever. Today we praise You in Your resurrection." In this way, the entire meeting will move forward and will be full of revelation. Therefore, praying in the table meeting involves many aspects. Our prayer may be compared to the four seasons, which can be represented by different kinds of blossoms. Our praises concerning the bread and the cup should change according to "the season." For example, even though we see the Lord's death, we are still in His resurrection.

Furthermore, the utterances of our prayer in a table meeting should not be too free or careless. For instance, someone may pray, "O Lord, You shed Your blood drop by drop." This is not appropriate. We may be able to teach in this way in a children's meeting, but we cannot pray like this in a table meeting. That would be a joke. Another example is to pray, "O Lord, our hands have sinned, so Your hands were nailed for us; our feet have sinned, so Your feet were nailed for us; our head has sinned, so Your head was pricked for us..." We may think that this is a good prayer, but this prayer is from the human mind and devoid of revelation. The Lord Jesus' hands and feet were nailed not merely because our hands and feet have sinned but because our entire being has sinned, including our ears, our eyes, our tongues, etc. Because of *Hymns,* #93, we can say to the Lord, "On the cross You measured sin's distance. When You were on the cross, You knew how far away we were from God because of sin. It was not until we saw Your death on the cross that we knew how far away we were from God because of sin. Before You died on the cross, we did not know how far away we were from God, and we did not even realize that we were sinners." This is a revelation.

In short, our prayers at the Lord's table meeting should focus on these six principles: being fitly connected, moving forward in the spirit, maintaining the feeling of the meeting, using poetic utterances, having revelation, and avoiding formal expressions.

CHAPTER SEVEN

A PRACTICAL EXERCISE OF PRAYING IN THE LORD'S TABLE MEETING

(2)

OFFERING STEADY PRAYERS

We may begin the table meeting with a hymn, follow the hymn with some prayers, and then sing another hymn. By this point in the meeting, the spirit should be relatively high and strong. When our praise has reached a climax, we should bless the bread and the cup. While the bread and the cup are being passed, if the spirit of the meeting remains very strong with the sense of the Lord in glory, another hymn might give us a feeling of being "out of breath." Hence, it is better to offer some steady prayers.

If the atmosphere of the entire meeting has reached a high point and we have been led to the subject of the meeting, with the bread and the cup having been passed, we should remain in a quiet spirit to be in steady fellowship with the Lord, meditating on Him and remembering Him. Selecting a hymn in such an atmosphere would disturb the meeting, causing it to lose its elegance. Therefore, it would be best for two or three brothers and sisters to stand up and pray. But the prayers should not be too excited because the meeting has already reached its peak. At this high point we need to remain steady and calm in an uplifted spirit and offer some words of praise so that the saints can sense the Lord's glory and sweetness. This is appropriate.

While we are exercising to offer this kind of prayer, we must remember to link our prayers with the bread and the cup and bring everyone's feeling toward the Lord's table. Our prayers should not be separate from the Lord's table; rather, they must be connected to the Lord's table. For example, when the bread and the cup are being passed, we can pray, "O Lord, as we take the bread and the cup, and as our hands touch the bread and the cup, we sense that You are the Lord of glory." In this way, we are immediately connected to the feeling and subject of the meeting and thereby enable the saints to touch something. This kind of exercise involves a great deal of learning.

PRAYING WITH REVELATION

Moreover, we should pray with words of revelation and avoid preaching prayers. What is a preaching prayer? And what is a prayer with revelation? Suppose we talk with two people concerning hall one of the church in Taipei. We may tell them that the meeting hall on Ren-ai Road is made of wood and has many glass doors and windows that face different directions. This is giving a sermon. However, we may bring them to hall one and say, "Look at the doors, the windows, the courtyard, and the inside furnishing." This is revelation, a seeing. One way is to give a sermon, and the other is to speak by revelation.

Suppose someone wants to find a wife for a brother. One day he visits the brother and says, "Brother, there is a Taiwanese sister; she is tall and has large eyes." This is giving a sermon. Then one day the matchmaker brings the sister to the brother and says to him, "This is Sister So-and-so." This is revelation.

Many times, our prayers are doctrinal prayers, not prayers of revelation. This means that when we pray, we merely recite a message to others concerning the Lord, as if the Lord is not there. We do not give others the feeling that the Lord is right in front of us and that we are gazing at Him while speaking of His glory. There is a great difference here. We need to have the utterance of revelation when we pray. Let us consider some examples: "O Lord, we praise You that You became flesh"; this is a doctrinal prayer. "Lord, thank You that today You are in glory, yet You still possess human nature. We praise You"; this is still a doctrinal prayer. "O Lord, although we are touching the bread, we sense You in glory. Lord, we praise You"; this is a prayer with revelation. Although these prayers refer to the same thing, they are expressed in two different ways. Whereas one is doctrinal and formal, the other is living and with revelation. Therefore, we must exercise to speak words of revelation. This is a great matter and should not be taken lightly.

There is no record of doctrinal prayers in the entire Bible. In Genesis 18 Abraham did not pray, "O God, You are righteous"; rather, he prayed, "Shall the Judge of all the earth not do justly?" (v. 25b). This is a prayer of revelation. Many brothers and sisters use doctrinal expressions and utterances in their prayers. Most doctrinal prayers lack poetic qualities, and many prayers of revelation are full of poetic characteristics. For example, the prayer, "Although You are in glory, what we see is the honor You received in glory," is somewhat poetic. It would be very good if all our prayers could bring us into the prayer for the bread and the cup of the Lord and if they also contained some poetic words of revelation.

PRAYING ACCORDING TO
OUR RELATIONSHIP WITH THE LORD

If we stand on our relationship with the Lord and pray according to this relationship, it is easy to pray with revelation. For example, we may pray, "Lord, You are in glory, but we are still here. O Lord, our eyes are still looking to the future. When You come back, we shall be with You in glory." With these few sentences we can touch something; it is as if glory has entered the meeting. It is not that glory has been transferred to us from eternity future; rather, the eternal glory is now intimately related to us. If we are afraid that the feeling of the saints is not strong enough or that our words are not clear enough, we may add a few sentences, "Lord, it seems that today only You are in glory and that we are not. But even now we know that the day will come when we shall be as You are; we shall be exactly like You." We need to give the brothers and sisters a feeling that the glory we enjoy today is not objective but subjective.

Our prayer should let the saints touch the Lord's glory. We

may pray, "Lord, You formerly walked on the earth, but now You are in glory, and You still possess human nature. Lord, because You still possess human nature, we can break the bread and drink the cup to enter into fellowship with You even though You are in glory. In such a fellowship, we remember You and we receive You. Lord, we worship You. If You were in glory but did not possess human nature, we would not be able to sense how dear and near You are to us. Lord, we praise You that You are in glory, yet You still possess human nature." Such a prayer brings our feeling into glory; moreover, this glory is seemingly objective but is actually subjective.

Therefore, we must come before the Lord to exercise to have utterance with revelation. We must touch the feeling of the spirit and have the utterance to express this feeling with revelation. With many of us, utterance in our prayer is a big problem. When we pray, it is difficult for us to touch the subject of the meeting or sense that the spirit of the meeting has advanced. The spirit of the meeting may be very high, but sometimes our prayers turn aside and do not touch the focus; if this is the case, it is difficult for us to maintain, to support, the spirit of the meeting.

PRAISING ACCORDING TO
THE FEELING OF THE HYMNS

Please remember that it is best for any prayers offered after a hymn to follow the feeling conveyed in the hymn. For example, *Hymns,* #136, "In Thy face once marred and smitten, / All His glory now we read. / Gazing on it we adore Thee, / Blessed, precious, holy Lord." When we reach a high point in the spirit in our singing, we need a prayer to sustain the spirit of the meeting. This means that the words, "Gazing on it we adore Thee, / Blessed, precious, holy Lord;... / Rise our hearts," have brought us to the high point. Then instead of praying doctrinally, we should focus on the last two verses and pray, "Yes, Lord, as we are gazing on Your face, our hearts rise up to praise You." Immediately this prayer is linked to the hymn. Then more prayers should continue to focus on the Lord's glory. The atmosphere of the meeting will then be such that everyone sees the Lord's glory in its utmost purity.

Hence, the author of the hymn does not need to say anything except, "Gazing on it we adore Thee, / Blessed, precious, holy Lord." If we can continue praising, the spirit of the meeting will be sustained. After numerous prayers of praise, our hearts will be fully turned to the Lord.

Then a brother may be inspired to add a short hymn and select the last stanza of *Hymns*, #182, which reads, "Praise Him! praise Him! praise the Savior! / Saints, aloud your voices raise, / Praise Him! praise Him! till in glory / Perfected we'll sing His praise." This is even better. After the short hymn, everyone may still have a lingering taste for the meeting; thus, we can send off the saints singing this praise once again.

If, however, there is still time after singing *Hymns*, #136 and offering prayers, we can sing hymns to fill the gap. *Hymns*, #141 is very good. It says, "Jesus, Thy head, once crown'd with thorns, / Is crown'd with glory now; / Heaven's royal diadem adorns / The mighty Victor's brow. / Thou glorious light of courts above, / Joy of the saints below, / To us still manifest Thy love, / That we its depths may know." It is very good to sing this hymn at the end of the meeting because it is very subjective. Stanzas 4 and 5 say, "Who suffer with Thee, Lord, today, / Shall also with Thee reign:... / To us Thy cross is life and health; / 'Twas shame and death to Thee; / Our present glory." On the one hand, it speaks of the Lord's glory, and on the other hand, it says that even though we have seen the Lord in glory, we are still on earth; we still need to follow the Lord in taking the way of the cross.

AVOIDING DOCTRINAL PRAYERS

We not only enjoy glory but also suffer shame, because today we are still on earth, and we need to despise the favor of the world. We should enter the path of the cross: "To us Thy cross is life and health; / 'Twas shame and death to Thee; / Our present glory, joy and wealth, / Our everlasting stay." In such a table meeting, we will have a feeling that we are already in heaven and that it is really wonderful. At this time there is need for prayer. Without a prayer the meeting cannot stand firm. We may pray, "Lord, we thank and praise You. We are full of joy before You; we have touched heaven and sense that we are really in heaven. O Lord, give us Your humility and authority that we may walk a little farther on the path of the cross." The center of such a prayer is correct; we have not only seen the Lord's glory, but this glory has become our strength to enable us to take the way of the cross on earth to go on with the Lord. But this prayer also contains very little revelation. Once a formal phrase such as "Lord, we thank and praise You" is used, the prayer is finished. Furthermore, this prayer contains too much asking. At this point the prayer should be an elucidation, an unveiling. The praying one may say, "Lord, now that we have seen Your glory, how can we not treasure the path of the cross?" This means, "Once we have touched this glory, we cannot but thank and praise You; we cannot but endure the shame of the cross." It would be doctrinal to ask the Lord for something in this prayer. The more we ask, the farther away we are. But if the sense of glory is disclosed, revealed, the saints will sense it, and we will not pray to enter into glory because we have already arrived in glory. This is the secret.

We would point out this way, hoping that the brothers and sisters will learn this secret so that in all kinds of meetings they will exercise to utter prayers of revelation, not prayers of doctrine.

CHAPTER EIGHT

A PRACTICAL EXERCISE OF PRAYING IN THE LORD'S TABLE MEETING

(3)

PRAYER BEING THE BEST WAY TO BEGIN THE WORSHIP OF THE FATHER

Some have asked whether we should first pray or first sing a hymn to begin the worship of the Father after breaking the bread at the table meeting. In practice, it is easier to begin with singing and more difficult to begin with prayer. If we are able to have a good beginning with prayer, it is best to begin with prayer. If the prayer is strong enough to touch the spirit of the meeting, even to touch this particular section of the meeting, then prayer is the best and the sweetest way to begin this section of the meeting. We should remember that this is the beginning of a section and not the beginning of a meeting. Thus, for the sake of spiritual elegance and height, it is best to begin with prayer.

It is best to use a hymn, not prayer, at the beginning of a meeting, because at the beginning the spirit is relatively low, and it is difficult to pray. In principle, however, prayer is the best way to begin, because a hymn is not as high as a prayer. But when we are unable to offer suitable prayer, we must use a hymn. After the breaking of bread, if the attendants are high in their spirit and able to follow the Lord Jesus to come before God, then it is not so good to start the worship of the Father with a hymn. We should have a prayer of continuity, a prayer that continues the flavor of the preceding section, that follows the Lord Jesus to come before God and to offer up praises to Him. Such praise turns the entire meeting from the first section to the second section, from remembering the

Lord to worshipping the Father. It would be very elegant and beautiful for us to sing a hymn after such praise and continue with two more prayers.

LEARNING TO TOUCH
THE ATMOSPHERE OF THE MEETING

The most precious point concerning a meeting is that we learn to touch the atmosphere, the feeling, of the meeting. Suppose the atmosphere of the meeting has already brought us to the point where we want to follow the Lord to take the way of the cross before us. This means that we have seen the Lord on the throne in glory, and we want to follow Him to take the way of the cross. In such an atmosphere, it would not be so appropriate for us to turn the meeting to enter into the worship of the Father by simply calling a hymn; this would not be elegant. However, if we can use a prayer to turn the feeling of following the Lord to an atmosphere of worshipping the Father, the praising spirit will be stronger, and we can then choose a hymn to express the spirit of praise and worship.

In such an exercise we still need to pay attention to the spirit and pay attention to praying with continuity. It is difficult to have the proper utterance for prayers in this section. For example, it is not proper for us to begin a prayer by saying, "O Lord." A prayer that begins with "Lord" is addressing the Lord, not the Father. Therefore, such a turn is not adequate. It is very difficult to make a turn after we have used the title *Lord*. If we call on the Lord's name in the section on the worship of the Father, the flavor will be weakened. Although God is both the Lord and the Father, when we speak of the Lord, we sense the aspect of His being the Lord; we do not sense the aspect of His being the Father. Thus, when we are worshipping the Father, it is best to call Him Father.

Our prayer should contain more revelation and fewer doctrines. Prayer is not preaching; rather, prayer is speaking forth a spiritual matter we have seen. Prayer is related to revelation, not doctrine. It is doctrine when someone tells us that the meeting hall is in such and such a condition. But it is revelation when he takes us to the meeting hall and shows us the glass windows and the planters.

A FEW PRINCIPLES CONCERNING PRAYER
IN THE LORD'S TABLE MEETING

How should we pray in the table meeting? If we firmly grasp a few principles, we will be able to offer proper prayers. First, there is "initiating" prayer, which means that the meeting does not have a particular subject, but we feel something in our spirit and express it with a prayer. For example, no one may have expressed a feeling concerning God's love, but one may have an inward, spiritual inspiration concerning God's love, a feeling that is as strong as an atomic bomb. If he expresses this feeling with a prayer, everyone will have a feeling concerning God's love.

Second, there is "expressive" prayer, which means that all the brothers and sisters have a certain feeling, such as the love of God; however, there is the need for someone to express this feeling with a prayer. This kind of prayer needs expressive utterance in order to speak forth this feeling. For instance, while sitting in the meeting, one may clearly sense that everyone has a feeling concerning God's love; therefore, he offers a prayer to speak forth, to express, this feeling. Whereas initiating prayer is for revelation, expressive prayer is a speaking forth, to pray forth the sense that is within everyone.

Third, there is "motivating" prayer. If we are in an atmosphere of remembering the Lord, but it is time to begin worshipping the Father, we need to be motivated in order to turn the atmosphere to the worship of the Father. Our spirit of worship cannot make a proper turn if we are not properly motivated; therefore, there is a need for motivating and strengthening. Previously the saints were in a spirit of remembering the Lord; now we should use a prayer to motivate, to draw out, the spirit of worship and strengthen it. Then we can go on to worship the Father. Thus, in the table meeting there are prayers for initiating, for expressing, for motivating, and for strengthening.

NEEDING TO HAVE A RESERVE IN OUR LIVING

I hope that we would all apply ourselves in these matters. If we have a personal reserve, we will be able to draw from it and use it in the meetings. Many times, we cannot open our mouths and pray, because on the one hand, we do not have the inspiration, and on the other hand, we do not have enough reserve. It is not that we lack a burden in our spirit to pray; rather, it is that we do not have the utterance for prayer or a reserve for prayer. For example, it may not be as easy for the Chinese to speak in English as it is for them to speak in Chinese. When they converse in English, they may not have enough vocabulary to express the many feelings within them; thus, there are many things that they cannot express.

In our daily living we must practice to gain the utterance for prayer; we also need a reserve of prayer. We do not merely need to exercise our praying spirit; much more, we must seize each opportunity to exercise out of our reserve of prayer. In this way we will gain the key to prayer.

PRAYER OF CONTINUITY

Some have asked what utterance and vocabulary are needed to pray in continuity. In the atmosphere of a meeting we may sense that we are before the Lord and that the Lord is among us; we also may sense that He is leading us and that we are following Him to the Father. At this time someone needs to create a feeling of praise to the Father and motivate and draw out the worship of the Father. After a motivating prayer, another brother should offer a prayer for strengthening. Then we need a prayer to express, not to initiate. To initiate something is to bring in something that was not present. However, when the spirit of the meeting is strong, and we all have the sense that the Lord of glory is among us and leading us to worship the Father, there is no need for an initiating prayer. There is only a need for an expressive prayer to continue the previous section.

Some of the prayers in the table meeting are initiating prayers; they speak forth a feeling that was not previously present in the meeting. Other prayers are expressive prayers to speak forth and express the feeling that is presently in the meeting. Still other prayers are motivating prayers to cause the meeting to turn from one atmosphere to another. Finally there are strengthening prayers. Regarding the words we use in our prayers, we should not speak doctrine; we should express the reality.

HAVING A DIRECTION IN OUR PRAYER

With the literature work in Shanghai we had a principle in writing our articles: we always considered that we were speaking a message instead of being shut up in a room alone. We would not have been able to write our articles if we considered ourselves as being shut up in a room. Even though we were writing in a room, we always considered ourselves to be speaking to an audience. Only in this way could our writing be living and real. Even though no one was with us, we considered that the brothers and sisters were before our eyes and that we were speaking to them.

Our prayer should be in this principle; we should direct our prayer. We know that the Lord Jesus is within us and among us; we are not simply praying to the air with our eyes closed. In this way we can be delivered from doctrinal prayers. I believe that our prayers will be greatly improved if we can firmly grasp these crucial points.

BEING DILIGENT IN OUR EXERCISE
AND NOT DESPISING IT

If we are willing to apply ourselves in these matters in the church life, we will be able to touch some definite, spiritual matters in the meetings. Our meetings are not rich or enjoyable because we do not know how to meet. For this reason we must carefully exercise how to meet; we should never consider this as a small matter. All who serve the Lord and all the responsible brothers in the churches must be diligent in this kind of exercise; we must not despise this matter.

CHAPTER NINE

THE STEPS FOR CHRIST TO BE FORMED IN MAN

Some saints are not clear concerning matters such as Christ's being in us and Christ's being in the church; therefore, we would like to have some fellowship focusing on their questions.

Question: How can such a rich Christ become the reality in the church and in the individual believers? How can He be formed in us quickly?

Answer: If a person is walking on the right path while pursuing the Lord, sooner or later he will see that throughout the ages God's work in His plan is primarily to work Christ into man, whether in creation or redemption. We should not say that no one has seen this matter in the last two thousand years, but we can say that very few have seen this. Man's natural concept and natural thought is his greatest problem before God. Christians must have the realization that man's natural concept is a problem that hinders Christ from living in them.

We each have our natural concept and natural view. After salvation, some saints think that it is good to never lose their temper, and others focus on the way of the church. There is nothing wrong with this. However, Christ can be hindered from living in one who regards the way of the church above everything else, because his firm belief in the way of the church may not be the result of revelation from God. Perhaps there is an affinity to the way of the church in his background, environment, and state of mind; thus, it is easy for him to comprehend and to accept the way of the church.

Hence, his understanding and acceptance of the way of the church is something natural and human.

Everyone who is saved should have a heart for the Lord, but the fact is that many do not have such a heart. There is no need to speak concerning the following matter with one who does not have a heart for the Lord. The Lord desires man to live by Him and let Him live in man so that man may live out His riches. The Lord has no way in one who does not have a heart for Him. However, the Lord also has a problem with those who have a heart for Him; this problem is their natural concept. We either do not love the Lord, or once we love the Lord, we think we should be zealous, humble, work diligently, preach the gospel for the Lord, fellowship with the brothers and sisters, and build up the church. Apparently these are good concepts, but in those who love the Lord, these concepts are the biggest enemies of Christ and hinder Him the most. Therefore, strictly speaking, even our eager expectation to live out the riches of Christ can possibly be according to human concept and therefore be the biggest enemy of Christ.

Let us consider, can we actually live out Christ by our eagerness? Can we live out Christ merely because we want to do so? This is a human concept. I am afraid that with many of us, our eyes have not been opened to see that "wanting" to live out Christ is a human concept, a human work. Man's "wanting" to live out Christ is actually an enemy of God. Whatever man "wants" to be and do originates from man himself, and this hinders Christ from being lived out.

There must be a day when God shows us that we have nothing, that we are good for nothing, and that we are devoid of any merit. Moreover, we must see that God's intention is to work Christ into us. First, we need to see that all of our concepts are useless. Regardless of how good our concepts are, they frustrate Christ from being lived out of us. Second, we need to see that God's intention is to work Christ into us. This is a revelation and a vision. We need to ask God to have mercy on us that we may have such a vision. Merely listening to man's preaching is futile. Once a person sees the vision, no matter who he is, he will prostrate himself before the Lord and stop all his speaking; he will no longer say that he will be good, zealous, humble, gentle, and diligent. We may be eager and try to study how to live out Christ, but we will be unable to make it in ourselves.

Question: What if we genuinely "want" to "let" Him live?

Answer: This is a mysterious matter. If one has a vision, "letting" works, but if one is without a vision, "letting" does not work. The shining upon Paul on the way to Damascus is a typical case (Acts 9:1-9). Before receiving the light, Paul was full of natural concepts in his service to God. He went to Damascus for the purpose of arresting Christians because he was exceedingly zealous for God. He did not have the thought, the intention, to sin or oppose God. On the contrary, he loved God and followed the footsteps of his forefathers to serve God in a pure conscience. However, after the shining of the light on the way to Damascus, his whole being was stopped, and he became blind. This means that he no longer had his own view and concept.

If we want to let Christ live in us, we must have a vision and a revelation. There must be a day when the Spirit of God shows us that the greatest hindrance to Christ's being lived out of us is our self. Our concept represents our self. We need to see this in order for us to stop our entire being. This does not mean that we do not need to pursue the Lord and love Him. We must still have a heart for the Lord and pursue to go on with Him. But in our pursuit of Him, we must stop ourselves. If we have the revelation of the Holy Spirit and truly stop our doing, allowing Him to work in us and to give us vision and revelation, we will see a strong twofold revelation. Such a revelation, on the one hand, will cause us to love the Lord even more fervently and, on the other hand, will cause us to stop our entire being, to stop our self.

We all love the Lord, we at least love Him a little, but we may have a bad temper. Hence, whenever we draw near to the Lord, we have the hope that our temper will be improved, and we therefore ask the Lord to help us. However, we need the Lord to open our eyes to see that even such a little hope is a natural concept that can be a hindrance to the Lord. We need to stop ourselves, but this is not an easy matter. When we see the light and receive revelation, we must stop ourselves; then we must give ourselves, consecrate ourselves, to Christ, not to do something for Him but to consent to His living in us. He cannot live in us before He has obtained our consent. We must agree with Him and give ourselves completely to Him.

We often have the thought of doing something for the Lord when consecrating ourselves to Him. When we give ourselves to the Lord, we frequently have a desire and make the decision to do something for Him. Very few consecrated ones do not have such a thought. In fact, nearly every consecrated one has an intention of doing something for the Lord. It is right for us to consecrate ourselves to the Lord, but we need to drop our desire to do something for Him. It is a natural concept, a human concept, to want to do something for the Lord, and it is this concept, this very thought, that frustrates Christ from being lived out of us. In our consecration we do not see that Christ is all and that He wants to live in us to be our all. Rather, we think that Christ needs our service and our work and that we are somewhat useful to Him. Such a thought becomes a hindrance to the carrying out of God's eternal plan in us. Although we have a heart for the Lord, when we have such a thought, we do not let Him have all the room in us.

Therefore, we must see that we are a problem to Christ. If we hand ourselves over to Christ without bringing along our own terms, desires, and intentions, He will be able to do what He desires in us. When we hand ourselves over to Christ, we should not hope that He will help us control our temper and make us gentle, nor should we pray that He will help us become useful in His hand and enable us to do something for Him. We should merely give ourselves to Him to be of the same mind with Him and to walk with Him, not having our own hope, view, and purpose but simply allowing Him to live in us. We need strong light from the Lord to show us that the way to enter into God's life depends upon our seeing these two points.

Question: What steps must we take before we can see these two points?

Answer: "It is not of him who wills, nor of him who runs, but of God who shows mercy" (Rom. 9:16). The eggs laid by a hen hatch and bring forth chickens because there is life in the eggs. If we have some imitation eggs that look exactly the same as real eggs, they will not hatch because they are void of life. Therefore, we can only say, "Be merciful to me, O God! Enable me to see that Your plan is for Your Son to be revealed in me, to be formed in me, and to fill my whole being so that He may live Himself out through me." It is only by revelation that we can see this. We cannot see it by exercising our will, by running, by wishing, or by thinking; all of these human efforts are enemies of Christ and hindrances to Him. We must stop ourselves. Today if Christians do not have a heart for the Lord, they will have no desire to do anything for Him. However, merely having a heart for the Lord is insufficient. A brother once asked, "Christ is rich, but why am I not rich inwardly?" It will not work and it will be useless for him to strive every day for Christ's riches to come into him.

Please bear in mind that while we should have a heart for the Lord, we should cease all of our efforts. People always like to ask, "What shall we do?" Whether in the Gospels or in Acts, from the time the Lord Jesus preached the gospel of grace, these questions were frequently asked: "What shall I do? How shall I work?" Then in Romans 9:16 Paul said, "It is not of him who wills, nor of him who runs, but of God who shows mercy." Romans 9 is the answer to all the questions. It is not a matter of "doing"; there is not such a thing as "doing." "Though the children had not yet been born nor had done anything good or bad…, it was said to her, 'The greater shall serve the less';…'Jacob have I loved, but Esau have I hated.'…'I will have mercy on whomever I will have mercy, and I will have compassion on whomever I will have compassion'" (vv. 11-15). After hearing this kind of word, if we can peacefully leave, saying, "Good! Let us all go home!" this may indicate that we have not been shown mercy. However, struggles may indicate that we have been shown a little mercy. Jacob struggled because he was shown mercy. But it was only when he stopped himself that mercy was fully manifested. However, when this one, who once held his brother's heel as a supplanter and a deceitful man, ceased his doing, God's mercy was manifested in him.

Perhaps not many can understand these words, but we believe that as long as these words remain in the church, one day they will shine upon some among us. We cannot comprehend these words in Christ by merely listening to a few messages. Jacob was shown God's mercy. But this was not fully manifested until he was at Peniel. There he wrestled with God; it seemed that God could not subdue him, but in the end God caused him to be crippled. Jacob loved God, but did he calculate according to God's calculation in the universe? He was so skillful that no one could prevail against him. He even struggled with God, but he was crippled when God touched the socket of his hip. From that day on God's mercy was manifested in him (Gen. 32:22-32).

God wants to work Christ into man, but man must stop his doing. No one knows how long it will take for us to stop ourselves; perhaps it will not happen until we are thirty, forty, or fifty years old. However, we should never think that some people are soft toward God. The fact is that we are all very hardened toward God. It is not easy for us to stop ourselves after only half a year or even a year; we need to pass through quite a long time. This is our real situation; we need to know ourselves.

Question: Does our stopping need to pass through the experience in Romans 7:25—"through Jesus Christ our Lord"?

Answer: We all know that when we preach the gospel, those who believe will be saved. However, if there are one thousand people listening to the gospel, not every one of them will have faith and be saved. Some gospel friends are still waiting, even after being repeatedly urged. This shows that even man's believing is the work of the Holy Spirit. Although we are responsible for preaching the gospel and for speaking, the Holy Spirit can work what we have preached and spoken into people. For example, I may be preaching the gospel on the podium; some in the audience may have come for the first time and others may have come several times. I may repeatedly say, "You must believe! You must believe!" Some may believe immediately, and others may not believe regardless of how much I say, "You must believe." Thus, whether a person believes is absolutely not dependent on our work.

Suppose we give a message that we must see the vision, consecrate ourselves, believe, and obey in order to let Christ live in us. After hearing this word, those who have been shown mercy will be enlightened, stop their entire being, and give themselves to Christ without reservation. This proves that the word entered into them. However, if a person has not been shown mercy, even if he can recite the points of the message about seeing a vision, consecrating himself, believing, and obeying, nothing will happen within him. Three or five years later the Holy Spirit may work in him, causing him to see the light. At that time he will clearly understand the message he heard earlier, and then he will stop himself.

God's mercy creates an opportunity for us to stop ourselves in the presence of Christ, and to realize that our behavior, our actions, and our desire to live out Christ are enemies of Christ. Even our good behavior and our actions for Christ are enemies of Christ, not to mention our bad behavior. When God causes us to see this, we will stop our entire being; we will stop ourselves thoroughly. This is not the issue of man's exhortation. We will not know the meaning of consecrating ourselves, giving ourselves to Christ, and letting Him live in us until a time of God's predetermination. Then we will clearly see that the faith in which we believe in Christ is Christ Himself. "The life which I now live in the flesh I live in faith, the faith of the Son of God" (Gal. 2:20b).

Question: Is it possible to enter into the experience of Christ's living in us immediately?

Answer: Some enter immediately, and others enter gradually. For example, with the experience of salvation some can say that they were saved on a specific date, but others, mainly those who grew up in Christian families, become clear regarding their salvation gradually. Andrew Murray is an example of one who gradually became clear of our need to stop ourselves. Andrew Murray, in his book *The Spirit of Christ,* repeatedly emphasizes that we must stop ourselves. Related to consecration, he does not say that we need to present something; rather, he uses the word *surrender* instead of *consecration.* This means that he was disarmed by Christ, defeated by Christ, and submitted himself to Christ.

This experience of Andrew Murray is correct. He mentions repeatedly our need to stop the activities of the flesh. When we truly have a vision of Christ, our entire being will be stopped, and we will see that Christ wants to live in us. Then we will no longer hope for patience and zeal. If we have seen that we can ride in a car, why would we want to ride a bicycle? Our entire being will be still when we see Christ; our zeal, patience, and humility will come to a halt, and we will completely surrender and submit ourselves to Him. We will say, "Lord, You are the Lord! You are the Lord of all, and all are Yours."

Whereas some see this immediately after they are saved, others see this gradually, beginning at the time of their salvation until they reach a certain point where they are thoroughly clear. From the autobiography of Andrew Murray, we know that he did not experience a sudden change. Even though he feared the Lord from his youth, he did not know on which day he was saved. He could only say that he realized he was saved and regenerated when he was in school. In *The Spirit of Christ* he does not clearly indicate on what day he saw that Christ lived in him. However, because he definitely saw that Christ lived in him, he could write this book; moreover, he already had a great deal of experience when he wrote the book.

We need to pursue having a heart for the Lord, a heart that loves Him, yet we should realize our pursuing and running are useless. This may sound contradictory. If our pursuing is useless, should we not stop pursuing? No, we must still pursue. On the one hand, we must pursue, but on the other hand, we need to realize that our pursuing avails nothing. We need to look to the Lord for His mercy that we might see. We should not believe that our zeal, diligence, or heart for the Lord are useful. These may help us work for Christ, but they cannot help us live out Christ. For us to live out Christ, our entire being must be stopped; even our being *for* Christ must be stopped. We must stop our entire being before Christ.

There are two sisters mentioned in John 11, Mary and Martha. In Christianity there is not an accurate understanding regarding these two sisters. Mary was not merely "quiet"; rather, she was one who stopped herself. Even though many people may be quiet, they cannot stop themselves. Martha was very active and also could not stop herself. Some sisters are very active; they are typical "Marthas." Other sisters are very quiet; they are seemingly typical "Marys." However, it is possible that both groups of sisters are "Marthas." Those who are quiet outwardly may not be still inwardly. In the meetings many sisters bow their heads and pray silently, but their blood cells are racing at top speed. Outwardly they are quiet, yet inwardly they cannot stop. In contrast, other sisters outwardly are running diligently, but their inner being is at rest. Hence, neither quietness nor activeness determines whether a sister is a Mary or a Martha. It is not a matter of whether one is quiet or active but of whether one has stopped himself.

Although saints everywhere are eager to attend revival meetings, we like to hold "calm" meetings. Our concept is radically different. I would be very concerned if someone has been stirred up by these messages or is very excited as a result of these meetings. This is because these messages are not to excite people but to cause them to stop themselves completely.

For over two hundred years, since the time of John Wesley and Count Zinzendorf, the churches on the European continent have taken the way of revival. In these two hundred years, many people have been raised up to do the work of revival. However, God also raised up a few who knew Him in a deep way. These ones repeatedly pointed out that the way of revival is not the best way for God to accomplish His purpose. The way of revival can bring people to salvation, but it cannot fulfill God's plan for the church. The way of revival can cause the church to increase in number, but it cannot cause the Body of Christ to increase in stature. For over fifty years we have been crying out to the saints who do the work of revival, saying, "We admit that your work has rendered Christians some help, but it cannot fulfill God's plan." Even though most saints care for revivals, we cannot do this work. Today the churches of the Lord do not need a work of revival but a work of revelation. We must let the Lord come in to show all who have a heart for Him what He wants to accomplish in His eternal plan.

When Paul wrote the book of Ephesians, he prayed that God would grant the saints a spirit of wisdom and revelation in the full knowledge of Him, in order that we might know what is the hope of His calling, what are the riches of the glory of His inheritance in the saints, what is the surpassing greatness of His power toward us who believe, and know the church as the Body of Christ, the fullness of the One who fills all in all (cf. 1:17-19, 23). Such knowledge cannot be obtained by being stirred up; it requires the revelation of the Holy Spirit. We can hold a three-day conference twice a year in which the saints continually shout Hallelujah. What happens after they have been "pumped up with air" in this way? We need to know that the faster air is pumped in, the faster it will leak out. After being "pumped up with air," some local churches are unable to continue carrying on their meetings; the work of revival always issues in this kind of result.

In mainland China a great number of people were saved through the revival work of John Sung, who is a perfect example of a revivalist. When John Sung conducted meetings, people would come and shout, "The precious blood of Jesus washes my heart, washes my heart, changing my black heart into a white heart." After ten days of such a revival, John Sung would leave and everything would leak away. Then Wang Ming-tao would come, and again the people, including the elderly and the young, would sing, "The precious blood of Jesus washes my heart, washes my heart, changing my black heart into a white heart." After Wang Ming-tao left, two months later the spirit would dry up and leak away, and the number of people attending meetings would also drop. Consequently, elders and pastors would meet to discuss the situation and then send a cable to invite Brother So-and-so from Canton. Once again, everyone would gather together to pray, to thank the Lord, and to praise Him. The church has been living a life of constant dependence upon revival meetings for the past two hundred years. This is like being addicted to morphine injections. The number of people in the church has increased, but the stature of Christ in the church has not increased.

We must ask ourselves: What are we doing here in Taiwan? Are we doing a revival work? Or are we providing a way for Christ to increase His stature in the church? We should never despise the preaching of the gospel to lead men to salvation. However, we should bear in mind that we should not pay attention merely to the preaching of the gospel in order to bring people to salvation while neglecting their knowledge of Christ after their salvation. The preaching of the gospel is to find material; the bringing of people to the knowledge of Christ is to build up these materials. The extent to which the saints can be built up and edified in the church depends upon how much we know Christ inwardly. For this reason I am not surprised when people speak with me regarding the situation of the churches, because I expect this. If the saints do not have an adequate inward knowledge of Christ, what else can be done other than revival works? We need the Lord's mercy that some among us will be enlightened by this word.

May God grant His church a spirit of revelation that the eyes of many of the saints will be opened. Our intention is neither to cause those who do not have a heart for the Lord to have a heart, nor to cause those who have a heart for the Lord to be more fervent. Rather, our desire is that some among us will be shown mercy and be enlightened. We should not pay attention to revival; we should change revival to revelation. We need revelation. The serving saints in all the localities need to see God's plan and how Christ is life in them. We need to see that we are the problem and frustration to Christ. We need to prostrate ourselves, stop ourselves, fully yield ourselves to Christ, absolutely surrendering to Him and giving all of our rights and ground to Him. No virtue can replace Christ, not even our zeal, patience, humility, or kindness; only Christ Himself is Christ. It is obvious that evil is not Christ, but neither is good Christ; only Christ Himself is Christ. Although we still live out goodness, the life that Christ lives out through us surpasses our goodness. We need to see this. This is what the Lord wants to do today. We should not despise the preaching of the gospel, but we need to pay attention to this revelation. I hope that we will all see this, pay attention to this, and spread what we have seen.

CHAPTER TEN

QUESTIONS AND ANSWERS CONCERNING THE PURSUIT OF LIFE

Concerning the pursuit of spiritual life, we should not take the easy way. As we are dealing with life, which is something living, we should avoid any dead condition. We should not focus merely on the principle of life; rather, we should focus on the genuine pursuit of life.

"HANDING OURSELVES OVER" NOT RELATED TO BEING STRONG OR WEAK BUT TO GOD'S ORIGINAL INTENTION

Question: How much of our need to "hand ourselves over" is related to our condition?

Answer: Since we have not had sufficient fellowship concerning this matter, many saints think that they need to hand themselves over because they are defeated. They seem to think that if they had not failed, that is, if they were all right, they would not need to hand themselves over. However, this is not the case. As far as God's original intention is concerned, we must still hand ourselves over no matter what our condition is, even if it is the best. Handing ourselves over has nothing to do with our condition. This relates to the fact that even apart from our sins the Lord needed to go to the cross and die for us in order to release the divine life. In God's eyes, even if we are strong and victorious, we need to hand ourselves over to Him for the divine life to be wrought and constituted into our being.

Humanly speaking, even if others consider our condition to be excellent, in the eyes of God we are still living out ourselves rather than the life of God. This is not what God wants.

God's intention is not to save and help us by His life because we are weak and our condition is poor. His original purpose in His plan is to work His life into us; this has nothing to do with whether we are weak or strong. When we are weak, He works His life into us; when we are strong, He still works His life into us. This is what He does whether we are weak or strong.

God needs our cooperation in order to work His life into us. However, His life being worked into us is not for making up a lack on our part. God's intention is to work His life into us so that His Son may be the Firstborn among many brothers for the expression of the glory of His Son. Since the light we have seen is inadequate, low, and shallow, we always think that we need the strong life of God to help us because we are weak. Actually, man needed God's life when he was still in the garden of Eden, long before our father Adam fell. This is typified by Adam's being placed in front of the tree of life after he was created. Even though Adam had not yet fallen and was not yet weak, he was placed in front of the tree of life in order to receive God as life.

Hence, we must hand ourselves over to God to let Him have the proper opportunity to work Himself into us so that His original purpose may be fulfilled in us. This is not related to being weak or strong; this is a matter concerning the accomplishing of God's eternal plan.

THE APPLICATION OF THE DEATH OF THE CROSS DEPENDING ON OUR SEEING LIGHT

Question: Subjectively speaking, do we experience the Lord's death once and for all?

Answer: Anyone with such a thought does not have much light. People analyze whether their experience of the cross is subjective or objective because they lack adequate light regarding the cross. They do not see that all things have been crucified with Christ, not just the old man and the flesh.

For a period of time there were two factors that caused me to be afraid of the Japanese; one factor was specific and the other was general. The general factor was that I had a bad impression of the Japanese; to my impression they were terrible. The specific factor was my being put in prison as a result of false charges brought against me by Japanese who were envious of the fact that the Lord was blessing my work in northern China. Even though I was released from prison because of a serious illness, I was still kept under surveillance. When I was released, the Japanese were in control, and Tsingtao was under their occupation. When I saw what the Japanese had done in Tsingtao, I was very depressed. One evening in 1945 a brother heard over the radio that the Japanese emperor would announce an unconditional surrender on August 14. I have not been afraid of the Japanese from the day I heard this news. Formerly, I feared the sight of a Japanese military officer. However, after hearing of their imminent surrender, I would not have been frightened even if they pointed a gun at me. This is to see a great light.

In the same principle, when the Lord opens our eyes to see that Satan has been defeated on the cross and that the cross has terminated all things, including us, then all that we are and have will be terminated. For three days, from August 13 through 15 of 1945, when Japan announced their surrender, some of us went everywhere, shouting, "Japan has surrendered! Japan has surrendered!" We were beside ourselves. We heard the announcement over the radio and read about it in the newspaper. It was not a matter of whether Japan's surrender was subjective or objective; it was a matter of seeing the fact that the problem between Japan and China was over.

The Bible tells us that Satan, sin, the self, our old man, and all things have been terminated on the cross. There is nothing subjective or objective regarding this. We should not think that objectively we need to know that our flesh has been crucified with the Lord, and subjectively we need to experience the crucifixion of the Lord when we are losing our temper. If we think this way, we may think that though we know that our flesh has been crucified objectively, it is difficult for us to experience it subjectively. This would mean that we need someone beside us to daily and subjectively remind us not to lose our temper. Once the news of Japan's surrender was broadcast, I realized that the Japanese were finished. From that time on I was not afraid whenever I saw a Japanese. Likewise, we need to see daily that our flesh has been crucified with the Lord. Perhaps we would say that we do not feel anything. This can be compared to my experience with the Japanese. Originally, I did not know that Japan had surrendered, but after a brother came and told me of their surrender, I was beside myself for three days. We need light that we may have a genuine seeing.

We need to hand ourselves over to God whether we are victorious or defeated. God wants us to hand ourselves over, because His original plan is to work Himself into us. Even in the beginning, in the garden of Eden, the created Adam was not weak and had not fallen, yet God still wanted him to receive the tree of life. If we genuinely see this great principle, we will not care for minor points. From eternity God's plan has been to work His life into us in His Son. We need to see this. This has nothing to do with our falling, sinning, being weak, or being strong. This is what God will do whether we are good or bad.

When we see this, we will forget trivial matters. It is a great matter to see that our condition does not matter; such a seeing can solve our problems. This also applies to Christ's death on the cross. We need to see that this all-inclusive death has been accomplished. On the cross, not only were we crucified, but the flesh, the self, and everything in the universe were dealt with by the cross. Death, Satan, and everything that was created was terminated on the cross. When Japan surrendered, all her people, including the emperor, great officials, and even small soldiers, were finished. As long as we see and receive Christ's all-inclusive death on the cross, our problems will be solved.

NOT NEEDING TO ANALYZE WHETHER OUR RECEIVING IS ACCORDING TO KNOWLEDGE OR THE SPIRIT

Question: Is there a distinction between receiving that is according to knowledge and receiving that is according to the spirit?

Answer: Concerning the declaration of Japan's surrender, was there a distinction between receiving this news as knowledge and receiving it by the spirit? When people heard of Japan's declaration of surrender, did anyone wonder whether he received the news as knowledge or in the spirit? We have these kinds of questions in our mind because we have not seen the Lord's all-inclusive death on the cross. Therefore, we ask ourselves: Is this subjective or objective? Is this knowledge or the spirit? Seeing is seeing. Japan's surrendering simply meant Japan's surrendering. Christ's death simply means that Christ died. His death which terminated all things simply means Christ's death terminated all things. The simpler we are when we apply these matters in our experience, the better. There is no need to analyze, because we cannot enter the spirit by analysis. The fact that Christ died means that Christ died; that all things were terminated on the cross means that all things were terminated on the cross; that we died in Him means that we died in Him. All analyses come from the mind.

TOUCHING GOD DEPENDING ON HIS MERCY AND OUR STOPPING DISTRACTING THOUGHTS

Question: Why is it that spiritual matters sometimes seem so real and at other times so distant from us?

Answer: This is exactly right. Spiritual matters can be very near, as near as "in your mouth and in your heart" (Rom. 10:8). They can also seem so distant that they are beyond our reach our entire life. This same principle applies to hearing the gospel and receiving salvation. One person may receive the gospel immediately upon hearing it the first time, whereas another person may not receive the gospel after hearing it numerous times. Suppose there are two brothers, and the younger one receives the gospel, but the older one does not. The older brother may ask the younger, "How did you receive the gospel?" The younger brother may reply, "I simply received it." The older brother says that it is difficult to receive the gospel, but at the same time the younger brother says that it is easy. This shows that God will have mercy on whomever He will have mercy, and He will have compassion on whomever He will have compassion (Rom. 9:15).

Our salvation is truly a matter of mercy. We are saved because God showed us mercy.

It is difficult for God to work in a person who does not think clearly. It is strange, however, that some people's minds are clear when we speak concerning subjects such as engineering, machinery, and economics. However, when we speak to them concerning God's salvation, no matter how hard we try, we cannot get through with them. They are easily distracted in their thoughts. This is truly a matter of God's mercy.

What can we do to receive God's mercy? If we want to give a lofty answer, we can say, "If God will have mercy on me, I will be shown mercy; if God will not have mercy on me, I will still ask Him for mercy." We need to be humble to say, "O God, enable me to see. Let me see today; if not today, then let me see tomorrow." However, our eagerness to see is often a hindrance to seeing. Yet at the same time a lack of eagerness to see can also be an obstacle. Hence, when the apostle Paul wrote Ephesians, he prayed for the saints, "That the God of our Lord Jesus Christ, the Father of glory, may give to you a spirit of wisdom and revelation in the full knowledge of Him" (1:17). Paul's responsibility was to write the Epistle, but whether or not the saints would know the Lord Jesus depended on God's mercy.

For this reason, whenever I give a message such as this, I am reluctant to exhort or incite people with words; by the Lord's mercy I would like to unveil this mystery so that perhaps some could hear and receive mercy to see it. Similarly, when we preach the gospel, we do not know who will be shown mercy. In this matter we can do nothing to help. Man's salvation is of God's mercy; no one can help in this matter.

We may think that we are very capable, but have we gained anything? We have preached the gospel, but our number has not increased. We have not gained what we thought we were capable of gaining. We need the light. In the book of Job, God did not speak until Job's friends had finished their speaking (38:1-2). When man stops speaking, the light comes. We are often bothered if we do not do something for the Lord, but even when we do, we often have no impact. This is because we do not have the light. God wants simplicity. Our words and thoughts need to be purified; they need the shining of God's light.

The most successful people in the world are the simplest people. This is the same in spiritual matters. We must stop our distracting thoughts and worship before the Lord, saying, "Lord, You are the Lord. Whether or not I see, You are still the Lord." Then our problem will be solved. We must be able to stop and not try to analyze whether something is this way or that way. If we think that we can find a solution by our analysis, we are finished. We need to learn to be simple. Since the Lord has said so, we should simply stop and receive. In response some might ask, "What if I receive it but nothing happens?" This continual asking of questions is like being presented with food but still asking, "Is there bacteria in the food? What if I eat it and have a stomachache? Should I see a doctor? What if the doctor is inexperienced?" Questions like these can be endless.

Many people are like this. They may have heard the words of the faith many years ago, but in their mind they have one question after another. Thus, they can neither touch nor receive the reality in God's Word. We need to stop our distracting mind, stop wandering in our mind, stop all our questions, and simply come back to God's Word to allow the light in God's Word to shine on us. Once we have the light and have seen the light, our being will spontaneously be terminated.

THE LAW, THE WORLD, THE SELF, THE FLESH, THE OLD MAN, AND ALL THINGS HAVING BEEN CRUCIFIED WITH CHRIST

Romans 6 shows that we who are baptized into Christ Jesus have been baptized into His death. We are a group of people identified with the death of Christ: "Knowing this, that our old man has been crucified with Him in order that the body of sin might be annulled" (v. 6). Galatians shows that "I," the flesh, and the religious world have been crucified. Galatians 2:20 says, "I am crucified with Christ"; 5:24 says,

"They who are of Christ Jesus have crucified the flesh with its passions and its lusts"; and 6:14 says, "The world has been crucified to me and I to the world."

Colossians 2:14 says that the ordinances were nailed to the cross, and verse 15 says that the rulers and the authorities of the air were hung on the cross: "Wiping out the handwriting in ordinances, which was against us, which was contrary to us; and He has taken it out of the way, nailing it to the cross. Stripping off the rulers and the authorities, He made a display of them openly, triumphing over them in it." This shows clearly that the law and the written ordinances were nailed to the cross.

Romans, Galatians, and Colossians list only a few items that are related to us. Since the believers in Rome were not clear regarding the significance of baptism, the apostle Paul asked, "Are you ignorant that all of us who have been baptized into Christ Jesus have been baptized into His death?" (Rom. 6:3). Then he went on to say, "Our old man has been crucified with Him" (v. 6). Because the Galatian believers tried to keep the law by themselves, Paul asked them why they still wanted to keep the law since they had already been crucified (Gal. 3:2-3). Since the Colossians wanted to go back to Gentile philosophy and the ordinances of the Old Testament, Paul told them that both Gentile philosophy and the ordinances of the Old Testament had been nailed to the cross (Col. 2:14, 20-23). Today our focus should be the crucified Christ, not the keeping of the law. Since the believers were not clear, Paul pointed out that the law, the world, the self, the flesh, the old man, and even all things have been crucified. The problems that occupied the believers in Rome, Galatia, and Colossae had already been terminated.

GOD'S WORK IN MAN BEING
FOR THE ACCOMPLISHMENT OF HIS PLAN
AND THE MANIFESTATION OF HIS WISDOM

Question: In the Old Testament God's work in man was outward, but in the New Testament it seems that God's work in man is inward. Why is God so complicated?

Answer: God spoke, and it was done; He commanded, and

it stood fast. This is the principle of God's creation. This is all that He needs to do in order to create. The principle of incarnation, however, is not the same. God established the types in the Old Testament before the New Testament age so that through these types men could comprehend the eternal purpose of God which is presented in the Old Testament. This purpose is to gain man and to accomplish what He wants to do in man. In the Old Testament whenever God wanted to call man to work for Him or whenever He wanted to move through man, it was always done through the Spirit of God coming upon man. In the New Testament in order for God to gain man, He gives the Holy Spirit to man and puts His life within man. Hence, from the day of our salvation, the Holy Spirit has been dwelling and spreading in us.

In God's creation He spoke, and it was done; He commanded, and it stood fast. But in order for God to accomplish His eternal goal, He had to pass through a process with numerous steps. This process is for the manifestation of God's wisdom. Therefore, the Old Testament presents types, and the New Testament presents the reality. In the Old Testament God worked on man outwardly, and in the New Testament God works on man inwardly. All of His work is for the accomplishment of His plan and the manifestation of His wisdom.

THE SALVATION GOD GIVES TO MAN IN HIS PLAN BEING A FULL SALVATION

Question: Is the salvation that we have received from God complete?

Answer: In the Old Testament age God gave the land of Canaan to the children of Israel. After they crossed the Jordan River, the entire land of Canaan was theirs. Their enjoyment of Canaan began when their feet stepped on the land. Even though they were able to enjoy only the part of the land they walked on, the entire land of Canaan was for their enjoyment. In the New Testament age the Holy Spirit has been in us from the day of our salvation. The Holy Spirit is Christ, and Christ is God. Thus, the Holy Spirit, Christ, and God are in us. But our knowing and enjoying the Holy Spirit depend upon our actual experience of Him. The day we were saved, we received everything, but we still need to hear the truth. The truth we hear points out and shows us that all that is in Christ is ours.

In God's plan Christ intends to work His glorious and great person into us. We received everything that Christ is at the time of our salvation, even though we did not understand this. Hence, God repeatedly sends His servants to tell us that all things are ours. Since we may not have heard clearly the first time, God arranges the environment so that we can have a better comprehension of what we have received when we hear it a second time. Since our knowledge and comprehension of salvation are very limited by our natural concepts, God gives us more of His divine speaking. This is the reason we have writings such as Romans, Galatians, Ephesians, Colossians, and Revelation in the New Testament.

This, however, is not to say that the riches of Christ were not our portion before we heard God's further speaking after our salvation. In fact, all the riches were our portion, but we did not know it. Hence, God in His Word reveals and shows that all things are ours, item by item. At the same time He shows that not only were we finished on the cross, but all things were dealt with on the cross. The only reason we think that we are poor is because we have not seen the full salvation that God has given us in His plan.

SALVATION DEPENDING ON GOD'S PREDESTINATION AND MAN'S RESPONSIBILITY

Question: What does "many first will be last, and many last first" mean (Matt. 19:30; 20:16)?

Answer: We should realize that there are always two sides to the truths in the Bible. The things in the physical world have this same principle. For example, our head has a front side with seven "holes" and a back side with no "holes." In the universe, according to Chinese philosophy, there are *yin* and *yang,* males and females, the sun and the moon. This simply reflects a law in the universe that everything has two sides. In spiritual matters, from God's side, everything is related to His mercy; from man's side, everything is related to man's responsibility. Let us consider the matter of salvation. From

God's side, if He had not predestinated us to enter His kingdom, we would be unable to enter, regardless of how much we strive and struggle. From man's side, if we would not believe and receive the gospel, we cannot enter the kingdom of God. Hence, some say that salvation is a matter of God's predestination, and others say that it is a matter of man's responsibility. There is no need for debate. From the side of God in heaven, it is God's predestination; from the side of man on earth, it is man's responsibility. D. L. Moody has said rightly that on the outside of the entrance to God's kingdom, it is written, "Whosoever will may come"; however, once inside, it is written, "Chosen before the foundation of the world." A student of D. L. Moody once asked him, "There is no doubt that salvation is predestinated by God, but when we go out to preach the gospel, what will happen if someone whom God has not predestinated believes?" Moody answered, "My child, just go ahead and speak. All who believe through your speaking have been predestinated by God." The same seed of life is sown into us, but in some it will bear fruit and produce thirtyfold, some sixtyfold, some a hundredfold, but some will not bear even twofold. This shows man's responsibility. To yield thirtyfold is good, to yield sixtyfold is better, to yield a hundredfold is the best, yet to yield nothing is the worst. This is the responsibility that man bears. Whether a seed can grow is God's responsibility, but whether a seed can be sown into man is man's responsibility. Whether or not God allows us to hear His word is His responsibility, but whether we receive His word is our responsibility. If we have a distracting mind, we will miss God's shining and will be unable to receive God's speaking. Therefore, we must stop our thoughts.

SPIRITUAL MATTERS DEPENDING ON "SEEING"

Question: The Lord Jesus was led by the Holy Spirit to be tempted by the devil (Matt. 4:1). Since we have received the Holy Spirit after believing into the Lord and being baptized, what should we do when the Holy Spirit leads us and evil spirits follow?

Answer: Many times, spiritual things may not be our reality; instead, they may merely be thoughts in our mind. Hence, we should look to the Lord in His presence and learn to stop these thoughts. We should not think that when the Holy Spirit leads us, evil spirits are always involved. The spiritual fact is that the Holy Spirit has been in us since the day we were saved and baptized. We should simply believe this fact, and spend more time to consider the Lord and draw near to Him, not allowing ourselves to be distracted in our mind about thoughts of evil spirits.

I have already said that in matters pertaining to our spiritual life, the most important thing is seeing. The Lord Jesus once said of the Jews that although they had seen Him in the flesh, they had not really seen Him (Matt. 13:13; John 12:40-41). If they had seen Him, they would not have forsaken and crucified Him. The reason the Jews crucified Him was that they had not seen Him.

There are three aspects of seeing. First, God must unveil the spiritual things to us. For example, if I am hiding something, you will be unable to see it unless I show it to you. If you want me to show it to you, you will either need to beg me, or, without your begging, I may voluntarily show it to you. If God does not show, unveil, His mysteries to us, we will be unable to see them. Hence, the first point concerning seeing is God's unveiling, showing, His mysteries to us. Christ is the mystery of God, and the cross is also a mystery. If God does not reveal Christ and the cross to us, none of us will be able to understand them. Thus, the first point about seeing is God's unveiling. It is only when God pulls open the veil in heaven, making known to us the heavenly mysteries, that we can know Christ and His cross.

Second, we need the veil taken away from our eyes that we may see. If we are blind, we will be unable to see anything. Hence, if we want to see, our eyes must be opened; they must be bright. If God unveils a certain matter to us, but we do not have eyes that can see, His revelation will be useless. In order for us to see what God has unveiled, our eyes must be able to see.

Third, there must be light. If we want to see an object, it must first be placed before us; then, we need eyes that can see; and finally, there must be light. Even if our sight is normal, we will be unable to see an object placed before us in the darkness of night. Hence, seeing spiritual matters depends on God's unveiling, our eyes being able to see, and God's shining. God's unveiling is His revelation. For example, Christ and the cross may have been mysteries behind the veil, but one day God will lift the veil and show us Christ and His cross. This is revelation. At this time our eyes must be open to see, and there must be the shining of light to enable us to see this spiritual matter. Therefore, revelation plus sight plus light equal seeing. Our seeing is called a vision. If our eyes are opened and God's light is shining, we will immediately see Christ when God reveals Him to us. This is a vision.

God has already lifted the veil in heaven. The problem is whether or not our eyes can see. Since God has given us revelation, He is surely willing to grant us light. There is thus no problem on God's side with the first and the third aspects. The problem on our side is that we may not have eyes that see. If we have revelation and there is light, we will not see anything if we do not have sight.

Many people have revelation but no vision, because their eyes are not opened. Many among us are blind, even though we have revelation, and the Spirit of God is doing a shining work here. This is our biggest problem. Whether we have eyes that see is our responsibility. Many of our concepts, views, and ideas are veils that hinder us from seeing. In order for the veils to be removed, we need to stop and reject all of our natural thoughts and ideas. Otherwise, we may think and think until the Lord comes back, and still be unable to see. If we do not stop analyzing, our eyes will be blurred, and we will not be able to see. Even if we do see, it will not be clearly. Some people in our meetings do not really want to see; they are satisfied with merely coming to the meetings. Thus, they see very little.

We must see that spiritual matters depend entirely on seeing. When there is seeing, there will spontaneously be believing, but without seeing, there cannot be believing. Once we see something, we cannot help but believe. Therefore, we need to remember that spiritual matters depend on our seeing. Christ is all-inclusive, but our experience requires that we have eyes that can see. If we have sight, we will see His all-inclusiveness; we will see that His death is all-inclusive and that His riches are all-inclusive.

DISTRACTING THOUGHTS HINDERING US FROM SEEING

Man's natural thinking is a big hindrance to God, because it restricts God. Spiritual matters are not for our study or analysis but for our eating, digesting, and receiving. We simply need to eat. Some people may ask, "What if we do not eat properly and become sick?" Such unnecessary questions hinder us from taking in what God has revealed to us. It will be difficult for us to see light if, after hearing a message, we ask endless questions. For example, a head chef may prepare a delicious dish for us, but instead of eating, we may ask, "Does the food contain bacteria? What if we become sick after we eat it?" What would the chef do? He would say, "I put out a delicious dish for you to eat, not for you to study." When some people see a "delicious dish," that is, when they hear a message, they do not analyze in their mind, rather, they open their "mouth" and take in everything spoken in the message, including the all-inclusive death of Christ and His all-inclusive riches.

We may use another illustration. After hearing a message concerning the four living creatures, represented by a man, a lion, an ox, and an eagle, some may ask, "What about fish?" As soon as they ask this question, everything that they have heard becomes null and void. None of the truths, not even the truth related to Christ or His cross, can enter into us if all we have are questions. This kind of situation is a "dead-end" street, and we will be filled with all kinds of strange ideas that are simply rubbish. We need to see that all these troubling and distracting thoughts hinder us from seeing clearly; hence, we do not have a vision.

Writers always like to make inferences, but it is altogether wrong to make inferences in relation to seeing a vision. We need to look to the Lord for His mercy and grace that we would have eyes to see, stop all our thinking, and simply receive what He reveals to us. When reading the Bible, we should stop all our thoughts in order to see. In the same way, when listening to God's word, we need to stop our entire being, including our natural thoughts, so that we may see the revelation in God's word. God has no way to show us anything if our mind is racing. The main reason that many saints are blurred in their vision is because of their distracting thoughts. When people speak to us, we should stop all our thoughts, even if we think that we are experienced; otherwise, we will be unable to hear what is being said. In order to hear, we must stop our natural thoughts. The reason we cannot see is that we have not stopped these distracting thoughts.

We need to go to the Lord and ask Him to grant us sight. We need adequate prayers, sight, revelation, and light. On God's side, there is no problem with revelation and light; on our side, however, very few of us actually have eyes to see and ears to hear. We do not need to study how to hand ourselves over, overcome the flesh, or be spiritual. Our need is to drop such questions and, instead, go to the Lord and say, "O Lord, I want to be as quiet and calm as You are. Grant me the light in this matter. Lord, I do not know what it is to be victorious or holy. I only know that I lack eyes that are clear. I look to You to enable me to see."

CHAPTER ELEVEN

QUESTIONS AND ANSWERS CONCERNING SPIRITUAL EXPERIENCES AND THE CROSS

GENUINE SPIRITUAL SEEING NOT OBTAINED BY FEELING

Question: I realize that it is wrong to say that we have not seen anything of the Lord's death on the cross, yet I feel that our seeing is not clear but rather blurry. I also realize the time of our seeing is not in our control; it is in God's hand. What is our responsibility while we are waiting for light? Shall we simply go on according to our blurred seeing even if we may fail?

Answer: Your problem is that you analyze too much in your mind. There are three parts to your question. You indicate that your vision is somewhat clear but blurry, that you have seen something but not enough. You want to know what to do before you see further. According to what you have seen, you think that you could fail and be discouraged, but you still want to go forward by faith. This shows that you are both clear and confused. You have seen something, but what you have seen is somewhat clear and somewhat blurred. Since what you have seen is not thorough or sufficient, you will fall, but after falling you will still want to rise up by faith. You are clear concerning these points. Your second question relates to what you should do before you see more clearly. Brother, you need to stop these distracting thoughts; these thoughts are the very reason you cannot see. The moment you stop this kind of thinking and analyzing, you will be able to see.

Seeing is the issue of three things: revelation, light, and

sight. Revelation and light depend on God; we cannot produce them. However, sight is our responsibility. Those who have eyes should see, and those who have ears should hear (Mark 8:18). This means that we are responsible for our seeing and hearing. We must confess that we already have revelation and light; now the responsibility of seeing lies with us. Are our eyes open or closed? Are they clear or blurry? Are they transparent or opaque? Are they focused or distracted? God is not responsible for the condition of our eyes. Rather, this responsibility is altogether on our side; we must bear it completely.

We may use an illustration. Suppose someone prepares a meal and sets it on the table; our only responsibility is to eat. No one can bear this responsibility for us, not even God; only we can bear this responsibility. The revelation is here, and light is here, but if we want to see, we need the light of God to shine on our inner eyes. However, according to our experience, we are easily distracted and disturbed. Our anxiety keeps us from seeing, our analysis keeps us from seeing, our knowledge keeps us from seeing, our slothfulness keeps us from seeing, our indifference keeps us from seeing, and our begging of the Lord keeps us from seeing. This is very difficult. If you want God to bear the responsibility for your seeing, you may pray, "O God, save me from all the distracting and troubling thoughts." But eventually, you need to realize that even after such prayer, we must still bear the responsibility for our seeing.

We should all be clear that spiritual seeing does not rely on our physical eyes or our soulish mind. If we rely on our physical eyes and our soulish mind to see spiritual things, we will be confused. This brother is confused in the matter of spiritual seeing because he has over analyzed his condition. Therefore, we must stop our distracting thoughts and learn to simply follow the light that the Lord has given us; the simpler we are, the better.

When we hear that the Lord's death on the cross has dealt with all things, we should simply bow our head and say, "O Lord, I praise You. Lord, I thank You." We should not analyze in our mind, saying, "I have seen only partially; I have not seen fully." It seems that no matter what we have seen and how much we have seen, we always analyze. Moreover, in our analysis we anticipate that we will be unable to stand but, instead, will fall and be discouraged. Nevertheless, we want to continue to stand by faith. Anyone who analyzes in this way will be hindered from seeing the light.

Perhaps I have not answered your question directly. But my response shows you that there is no need to answer your question. In order to answer your question, we would need to sit down together. Otherwise, I would answer the first question, then after this I would answer another question, and then I would answer yet another question. There would be question after question, but in the end, even after I have answered all the questions, we still will not be able to see. There is not a problem with the questions that are asked but with the person asking the question. You must stop your analytical mind; do not analyze any longer; stop all of your distracting thoughts. You need to simply receive what you have seen.

In fact, genuine seeing is not related to any feeling. For example, at the time of our salvation, we opened our heart and received the Lord Jesus as our Savior. But at that moment, we did not feel that the Lord Jesus had entered into us, nor did we feel that there was something in us causing us to be joyful and radiant. Very few believers have a realization of being joyful and radiant immediately after receiving the Lord. Some have this kind of experience, but it is not necessarily typical. Rather, when we look back after a period of time, we realize there was joy and radiance. Therefore, we should not think that we have not received anything simply because we did not have an overwhelming experience. Rather, we did receive, but we simply did not have great feelings.

For example, after hearing a message a brother may not have a strong feeling concerning what he saw, yet he does not analyze. He simply feels that he is full of the Lord's presence. Before arriving home, he neither feels nor sees that all things have been terminated. However, a test comes when his wife loses her temper with him. As he is about to respond, he immediately senses something within telling him to die. He does not know how this sense entered into him. Only later does he realize that this sense was the all-inclusive death of Christ.

On the contrary, another brother is excited and joyful after listening to the message, because he has clearly seen that he has been crucified with Christ. On his way home, he tells the people in the car, "I have seen it." When he arrives home and his wife loses her temper with him, he tells himself that he must not react because of what he has seen. This type of seeing is in the mind, not in the spirit. When food enters our stomach, are we in control of how long the food will stay in our stomach before entering the intestines? Does it do any good to rebuke the food for lingering too long in our stomach or to tell it to enter quickly into the intestines? The Lord, who is in us, bears the full responsibility for us, and His word of life is like a seed that is sown into us. Although we may not know or feel it, once this seed comes into us, it begins to operate within us. We do not need to teach or remind ourselves; we do not need to say repeatedly, "I have seen it, so if my wife loses her temper with me when I go home, I must always remember that I have seen this fact: I have died with Christ. Therefore, I must not lose my temper."

Spiritual seeing is inwardly clear and outwardly blurry. If a brother comes to us and says that he has the faith and the seeing, his faith and seeing are surely man-made. In brief, spiritual faith cannot be described. What one believes can be described only after he looks back at his experience. When he is in the middle of the experience, he is altogether unclear. Please bear in mind that spiritual seeing cannot be understood by analysis. The more a person analyzes, the more difficult it is for him to see. Spiritual seeing is not a mental exercise; it does not depend on our theoretical analysis and understanding. Rather, spiritual seeing lies in the fact that a reality, something real, has comes into us.

Those who analyze with their mind often think that they are clear, but actual seeing does not necessarily involve much feeling. When we are in the midst of a spiritual experience, we often are not clear. The more genuine a spiritual experience is, the less clear we are throughout the process. However, if we are clear from the beginning of an experience, our seeing is questionable. In order to have genuine seeing, there must be a suitable condition, inwardly and outwardly, for God to shine in us, for the seed in God's word to be planted in us, and for the seed of God's life to be sown in us. When this seed is sown, we may call it seeing or receiving, and we may also say that this seed has been sown or shined into us. In any case, a certain spiritual matter has transpired within us. Once this spiritual matter is sown into us, it becomes our inward seeing. Even though we may not have any feeling outwardly, within us there is a spiritual fact that cannot be denied, nullified, or overthrown.

Although what is sown into a brother may not give him much feeling, when his wife loses her temper with him, it will be manifested; he will sense that there is something within that kills him and prevents him from talking back to his wife. At this time, he will sense that there is an additional element within affecting him. He may not know when this element entered into him, that is, he does not realize if it came into him when he heard about the cross and the all-inclusive death of Christ or if it entered into him later. An even better example would be that when he is face to face with his wife and his wife rebukes him, he does not talk back to her loosely but later simply thanks and praises the Lord, without any realization of the killing of the cross. This is the best experience. Even though he does not feel it, there is something real in him.

Let us consider eating as an example. When food enters into us and supplies us inwardly, we do not have much feeling; it is at a time of hunger that we have feeling. The more normal a spiritual matter is, the less feeling we will have in our experience. When a spiritual matter enters into us, outwardly speaking, we do not have any feeling. But when we have a need, this spiritual reality in us will meet the need. If our situation is normal, we may not even have a feeling when a need is met within us. For example, a brother may be inwardly stopped from talking back to his wife after she scolds him. He may not realize that it is the Holy Spirit activating the effectiveness of Christ's death on the cross within him. But when he looks back before the Lord, he will realize that this was an experience of the cross.

THE VEIL BEING TAKEN AWAY
WHENEVER THE HEART TURNS TO THE LORD

Question: In Acts 9, when the apostle Paul met the Lord on the way to Damascus, did the Lord appear to him inwardly or outwardly? Then in 2 Corinthians 3:16, Paul says that whenever the heart turns to the Lord, the veil is taken away. In order to have the Lord's appearing, must we first remove our veil, or must the Lord work in us first?

Answer: If we were to ask Paul whether he saw Christ when he saw the great light on the way to Damascus, or whether he saw Christ later when he wrote 2 Corinthians 3, he would definitely say that he does not know. He only knows that he met the Lord on the day when he was on the way to Damascus. After he met the Lord, what was formerly clear to him became blurred. Formerly his eyes were bright, but now he was blind. If we were to ask Paul where God revealed His Son in him, he would say that it was in Damascus at the time Ananias laid his hands on him. Paul could say that although it was Ananias who laid his hands on him, from that point on, it was God who revealed His Son in him. This is good enough. We really do not need to study whether the scales fell from his eyes first or whether the Spirit of Christ entered into him first, because Paul himself was not quite clear. If we engage ourselves too much in this kind of study, we will easily be blinded. This is an insignificant thought, which greatly frustrates us from seeing light. The story of Paul on the road to Damascus simply shows that we need to be met by the Lord before we can meet Him inwardly.

Second Corinthians 3:16 says, "Whenever their heart turns to the Lord, the veil is taken away." This shows clearly that if our heart does not turn to the Lord, a veil is there. The veil is taken away not by God's removing it but by our turning our heart to the Lord. Actually, our turned-away heart is a veil. What is a veil? A veil is something that hinders us from seeing. If I am face to face with you, and there is a veil between us, I cannot see you. But if the veil is taken away, I can see you. If I turn my back toward you, I cannot see you; this is to be veiled. But if I turn toward you, I can see you, and there is no veil between us.

Similarly, as soon as we turn around and look at the Lord, we will see the Lord. Not facing toward the Lord is the veil, but once we turn toward the Lord, the veil is gone. Whenever our heart turns to the Lord, the veil is taken away. The children of Israel began to have the veil from Mount Sinai. The veil that Paul spoke of in 2 Corinthians 3 does not refer to an outward, visible veil but to an inward veil which obstructs man from seeing God's glory.

With the children of Israel, the veil came in at Mount Sinai. The veil came in because the children of Israel began to rely on themselves when they were at Mount Sinai. God said, "I bore you on eagles' wings and brought you to Myself. Now therefore if you will indeed obey My voice and keep My covenant, then you shall be My personal treasure from among all peoples, for all the earth is Mine" (Exo. 19:4-5). Then all the people answered together and said, "All that Jehovah has spoken we will do" (v. 8). From that time on, a veil came upon the children of Israel and remains on them until now (2 Cor. 3:15).

Then in verse 16 Paul says, "But whenever their heart turns to the Lord, the veil is taken away." The principle is the same today. In Matthew the Lord said, "Blessed are the pure in heart, for they shall see God" (5:8). To be pure means that we want only God, and we do not want anyone or anything besides God. God is light (1 John 1:5). If our heart is facing toward the Lord, we will have light.

THE CROSS BEING GOD'S PROCEDURE
FOR REACHING HIS ETERNAL GOAL

We must see that with the Lord Jesus, He first bore the cross and then was crucified; but with us, we first are crucified and then bear the cross. The Lord's living on the earth began with bearing the cross and ended with crucifixion. Our living—the Christian living—should begin with crucifixion and continue with bearing the cross. In other words, our Lord took the cross and bore it the moment He was born on earth, and He continued bearing the cross for thirty-three and a half years. He never lived a life apart from the cross. However, we should not understand the cross merely as a suffering; at the same time, we should not consider that the Lord was ever free from suffering during His thirty-three and a half years on earth. The significance of the cross is death and termination. Throughout the thirty-three and a half years of the Lord's living on earth, He was never freed from death. He served God by standing in death day by day. He stood in death and lived in death. In those thirty-three and a half years, He always bore in His body the brands of death. He was in death, He lived in death, and He did the work of God in death.

In the end He was crucified, and before the entire universe He thus displayed the death He had borne for thirty-three and a half years and accomplished the fact of His death. From the day the cross was displayed, His all-inclusive death has become a glorious fact in the universe. This fact includes you and me and all the created things.

There is one goal in God's plan, and this goal is Christ. The cross is God's procedure for attaining the goal. His death on the cross is a great "surgery," because the entire universe was crucified and dealt with by Him. Everything has been dealt with on the cross, whether it be the angels, Satan, or man. That was a great "surgery." The unique and greatest surgery in the universe is the cross through which God reaches His goal. The cross is the procedure that God needs for His eternal plan.

In order to carry out this procedure, one day Christ became flesh; He came to be a man, joining Himself with His creatures. The process of His death was not completed when He was born into humanity; it merely became a possibility for Him. Hence, He Himself first lived in that "surgery"—death. Even though His physical death was not yet accomplished, He was already living in it for thirty-three and a half years. At the end, He carried out the actual procedure of death on the cross at Golgotha. What He did on the cross that one time fully accomplished the procedure foreordained in God's eternal plan.

Our Lord can be compared to the best cook who, after preparing a meal, makes it available for us to enjoy. On that day the Lord Jesus accomplished death for us on the cross and made it available for us to receive. If He had not died on the cross, He could not have made His death available for us to enjoy, even though He lived His life in death. For thirty-three and a half years, only He was in death. Peter could not enter into His death, neither could John nor James; no one could enter into His death. It was not until the day His death was accomplished on the cross that His divinity, humanity, human living, and all-terminating death could become our enjoyment through His resurrection life.

BEING CRUCIFIED WITH CHRIST IN HIS RESURRECTION

From that time Christ in His resurrection has become our life. He brought His death and resurrection into us, completing the work of the cross that we need to bear. God in His eternal plan determined to perform a great "surgery" to terminate all things through the death of the cross. This death was produced through Christ becoming flesh, becoming a grain that would fall into the earth and die (John 12:24); this is the first step. After He became this grain, for a period of thirty-three and a half years He bore this death and lived in it. The Bible repeatedly shows that His death has terminated everything outside of God. This is the cross the Lord Jesus bore.

For thirty-three and a half years, this death was the cross that He bore. Although the Lord Jesus experienced this death, it was not yet an accomplished fact in the universe. For example, a man and a woman may love and trust each other, but as long as they are not married, they are not a couple. Once they are married, however, their marital relationship becomes a fact in the universe. In the same way, although the Lord Jesus lived in death, this death was not displayed or accomplished as a fact, a procedure, in the universe. Hence, after thirty-three and a half years, He went to Golgotha to fully accomplish this death; then He transmitted it to us in

His resurrection. Only in His resurrection can we enjoy His death. In His resurrection we partake of Christ and all that He has accomplished.

Hymns, #481 says, "'Tis not hard to die with Christ / When His risen life we know" (stanza 2). What a statement this is! Christ in resurrection has become our enjoyment. When Christ was raised from the dead, He gave His life to James, Peter, and John. When we receive the resurrection life of the Lord, this resurrection life becomes our life. The Lord Jesus first bore the cross, and then He was crucified. Once the death of the cross was accomplished, He gave His life to us through resurrection. We were crucified with the Lord Jesus. We were crucified at the same time that the Lord Jesus was crucified.

Because the Lord has given us His life of death and resurrection, this life causes us to be united with His death. In His crucifixion He included us in His death. After He was crucified, we did not leave the cross. From that day forward, we receive the cross in the resurrection life; from that day forward, the cross has been on us and in us, and we are continually under the cross. This is to bear the cross. Bearing the cross is based on our crucifixion with Christ. He first bore the cross and then was crucified; we first are crucified and then bear the cross. Our crucifixion and His crucifixion transpired simultaneously. This shows that the Lord bore the cross before He was crucified; He was crucified after He bore the cross. Today we still have the cross upon us. Whenever the cross is not upon us, the death of Christ is not upon us.

THE CROSS GIVING US A DEEPER SEEING

Question: Is there a higher experience related to the cross?

Answer: One day I was going to invite a brother to have fellowship about the problems he had in serving the Lord. Right after I decided to invite him, death began to operate in me. The operation of death asked me inwardly, "Concerning your invitation, who is inviting him, you or God?" As the cross was operating in me, I immediately asked myself, "Am I inviting him, or is God inviting him?"

We need to see that the cross does not merely touch our behavior; it works so deeply that it touches us even in the matter of serving God. This aspect of the killing of the cross is not as simple as the killing that we experience when we are about to lose our temper with our family or when we are watching a movie; that kind of killing is too low. When we want to work for God, the cross operates in us at a higher level, asking, "Is this of you? Or is it of God?" If the cross checks us inwardly, we must submit to it immediately and say, "O Lord, I will not invite the brother." In such cases, we need to be able to bow our head and say, "Lord, I do not want any element of myself to be here." Therefore whenever we are about to speak to a brother, there will be an inward operation, asking, "Does this word come from you or from God? Is it just for your own interest?" This is the operation of the cross.

Once day the Holy Spirit will reveal to us the universal death of the cross. Once it enters into us, it will begin a deep operation that not only touches us regarding our outward behavior but also gives us a deeper seeing. This is a higher experience of the cross. Our deliverance from the self and denying the self must be the issue of the work of the cross, because in ourselves we have no way to be delivered from the self and to deny the self. To be delivered from the self and to deny the self altogether depend on our receiving the work of the cross.

THE DEATH OF THE CROSS AND
THE DISCIPLINE OF THE HOLY SPIRIT

Question: What is the difference between the killing of the cross and our submission to the discipline of the Holy Spirit?

Answer: Anyone who is not on the cross cannot submit to the discipline of the Holy Spirit. Only those who live in the death of the cross can submit to the authority of the Holy Spirit, the discipline of the Holy Spirit, and the environmental dealings of the Holy Spirit. For thirty-three and a half years the Lord Jesus lived in death and under death. Death left a mark on Him; He carried the brands of death with Him and never departed from death.

Because death was always with the Lord Jesus, He could submit to the ruling of God continuously. We are identified with Christ's death in the resurrection life. This death in the resurrection life enters into us, operates in us, and enables us to submit to the authority, the restriction, and the dealings of the Holy Spirit. In this way, when we receive dealings in the environment, not only are we without murmuring, but we also rejoice. Anyone who does not live under the death of the cross cannot live under the discipline of the Holy Spirit.

There was a sister who was always submissive; she would do whatever she was told. However, although she was submissive and would do whatever people asked her to do, she would murmur afterward. When someone said, "Sister, please wipe the chairs," she would wipe the chairs with smiles. Afterward, however, she would murmur and say, "Why did you not ask someone else? Why did you choose me?" I had never seen her refuse a request, but neither had I seen her do anything without murmuring. Although she was willing to accept all kinds of arrangements, it was always accompanied with murmuring. Outwardly she would accept and receive the arrangement with smiles, but inwardly she would murmur. Then when she saw someone close to her, she would say, "The brothers' arrangement is too much to bear." Her initial response was apparently submissive to the authority of the Holy Spirit, but actually it was not. Only those who live under the death of the cross can submit to God and say from the bottom of their heart that every arrangement of God in the environment is sweet and pleasant. Only such ones are really bearing the cross.

Bearing the cross began with Christ's crucifixion. Our bearing of the cross is based on His crucifixion. He bore the cross to Golgotha, and His death on the cross was sown and imprinted in us. Hence, our way does not depend on asking or begging but on seeing that we have already died on the cross and have no way to escape His death. Taking the way of the cross in death involves neither being humble nor suffering. Whenever we touch this death, we touch Christ, we touch life, and we touch the Holy Spirit. At the same time we also touch the defeat of Satan and the losing of sin's power.

In the death of the cross we see that all that the cross has accomplished, delivered, solved, judged, and dealt with is our portion.

THE DEEP MYSTERY OF A CHRISTIAN

Question: When the Lord Jesus was on the earth, He was obedient even unto death. Do we also need to be obedient unto death?

Answer: The Lord Jesus first bore the cross and then was crucified; He was obedient unto death. We, however, are crucified and then bear the cross; the bearing of the cross also requires obedience from us. When we believe in the Lord, the first thing we need to do is to be baptized. This means that once we receive the Lord as our Savior, the first thing we need is to be baptized. What is baptism? Romans 6:3 says, "Are you ignorant that all of us who have been baptized into Christ Jesus have been baptized into His death?" The first thing that God wants us to do, after receiving the Lord, is to enter into the death of the cross of Christ, to be baptized into His death. After baptism, we must begin to take the way of obeying the Lord. After we believe into the Lord, we need to be baptized; after baptism, we need to begin living a life of obedience and taking the way of obedience. This obedient living begins with Christ's resurrection. After we believed in the Lord, He put us into the death of Christ, and from that point forward we could begin to obey God.

After baptism, however, many people turn from the Lord's death and do not bear the cross. Not bearing the cross means that we are not living in the death of the cross. If we have seen what it means to be baptized into Christ's death, we will know that we are in the Lord's death, and this death has been wrought into us even after our baptism.

For example, a renowned doctor of chemistry, who had a strong mind having read many books and having studied in Germany, believed in the Lord. Then we told him that he needed to be baptized and that the meaning of baptism was to die and be buried with Christ. The day after his baptism, we saw him again and talked about his believing in the Lord. As we began our conversation, his doctor-of-chemistry mind began to come out again. But immediately after saying, "I think," he stopped himself.

From his fellowship with the brothers he knew that believing in the Lord is to be joined to the Lord and to fellowship with Him, and that being baptized meant to die and be buried. On the day of his baptism, God shined a mysterious light into his being. The next day when he was about to express his opinion, he could not continue. Death was operating in him, saying, "I thought the *I* in *I think* was buried. Why are you trying to come out of the tomb?" After this he could only say, "O Lord, what do You think? What will You say? It is no longer I but Christ. It is no longer I that live, but it is Christ who lives in me." The words he sang in his baptism, "Already dead! And buried too! / With the old man I am through!" (*Hymns,* #938), was not merely a saying but a revelation which was sown into him and was operating in him so that *I* and *I think* would no longer be expressed.

He did not live by man's exhortation; he lived by the spiritual reality of death. This is the way of a Christian, and this is the need of a Christian. Asceticism is futile; neither does devotion avail anything. The way of a Christian is the seeing of "death"; the way of a Christian is death. Hence, we need to bear in mind that death is what God accomplished and it is the mark of the Christian life. The Christian life begins with baptism, and the meaning of baptism is that we leave, and Christ comes; we are finished, and Christ begins; we die, and Christ lives. This is not only the case on the day of our baptism; it will be this way to the last day of our life. Only those who know the death of the cross of Christ know the deep mystery of being a Christian.

LEARNING TO STOP AND RECEIVE LIGHT

Question: Is seeing progressive? Is the degree to which we see the degree to which we stop?

Answer: The first thing is not to see but to stop. Of course, there are some stronger ones who first see and then stop, but ordinary people generally stop first. Saul of Tarsus, a well-known person throughout the centuries, was breathing threatening on his way to Damascus. There were some people he wanted to seize and others he wanted to kill. However, the shining in Damascus subdued him. Once the light shined upon him, his entire being stopped. Previously he led people, but now he had to be led. Moreover, because his eyes were blind, he had no choice but to stop. When we pause, God's light will be able to shine in us. If we are willing to stop for a little, God's light will shine in us a little; if God's light shines in us more, we will see more. The more we see, the more we will stop; the more we stop, the more we will see. This is the principle.

In church history Andrew Murray was a good example of one who saw gradually and stopped gradually. In his writings he often spoke of being quiet and fearful. When we stop ourselves a little, God will speak to us a little; if we receive His speaking, we will continue to stop ourselves. Hence, it is exceedingly important for us to learn to stop our mind before the Lord.

TWO ASPECTS OF THE WORK OF THE HOLY SPIRIT NOT BEING SEPARATE FROM THE CROSS

Question: Does the cross have a positive aspect? As far as the experience of the cross is concerned, is the filling of the Holy Spirit an inward filling or an outward pouring?

Answer: The cross has two aspects, a positive aspect and a negative aspect. On the negative side, the cross is for termination; on the positive side, the cross is for life dispensing. All of our experiences of the Holy Spirit must pass through the cross. After the Lord's crucifixion the Holy Spirit was manifested on the evening of the day of the Lord's resurrection and on the day of Pentecost. Two events transpired on two days. On the evening of the Lord's resurrection, the Holy Spirit as breath was breathed into man as life (John 20:22); on the day of Pentecost, the Holy Spirit as wind came upon man as power (Acts 2:2-4). Many people acknowledge the aspect of the Holy Spirit seen on Pentecost but not the aspect of the Holy Spirit seen on the evening of the Lord's resurrection. Even Andrew Murray was not clear regarding this point. He had the experience, but he was not clear regarding the truth. He said that the experience of the indwelling Spirit is the same as the experience of the outpoured Spirit, and the experience of the outpoured Spirit is the same as the experience of the indwelling Spirit. This proves that he was not clear concerning the two aspects of the work of the Holy Spirit. From his writings we can see that he was confused in the experience of these two aspects. According to the truth, it is one thing for the Holy Spirit to dwell in man, and it is another for the Holy Spirit to come upon man. On the day of the Lord's resurrection, the Lord breathed into His disciples and said to them, "Receive the Holy Spirit" (John 20:22). Therefore, we cannot say that they did not have the Holy Spirit. Forty days later, however, the Lord told them that the Holy Spirit had not yet come and that they were to wait for the Holy Spirit (Acts 1:3-5). This shows the two aspects of the work of the Holy Spirit. Although there are two aspects, there are not two Spirits but one Spirit with two aspects of work.

Revelation further tells us that the Spirit is now the seven Spirits (1:4; 3:1; 4:5; 5:6). Are there actually seven Spirits? No. There is only one Spirit, but this Spirit is intensified in function sevenfold. From the Bible we can see that the Holy Spirit has several aspects in His work. His descending upon us is one aspect, and His being breathed into us is another. His being breathed into us is for us to receive life; His descending upon us is for us to receive power. Both of these aspects came into existence after the Lord's crucifixion.

Thus, without passing through the cross, there is no way to reach a "day of resurrection," and without passing through the cross, there is no way to reach a "day of Pentecost." Without passing through the cross, it is difficult to receive the Holy Spirit into us as life, and without passing through the cross, it is difficult for the Holy Spirit to come upon us as power. The cross is necessary to experience these two aspects of the Holy Spirit. Not a single experience of the Holy Spirit can bypass the cross. There is nothing that God wants to do in us that can be separated from the cross.

THE WAY OF A CHRISTIAN
BEING TO ALLOW THE CROSS TO WORK

Question: What is the operation and work of the Holy Spirit within us? What is it to feel oppressed inwardly?

Answer: All the problems in our spiritual experience need to be dealt with by the cross. The problems in our mind, emotion, and will need to be dealt with by the cross. This means that the more we know the cross, the more the cross can do a killing work within every part of our being. When we are in our mind, the death of the cross deals with our mind; when we are in our emotion, the death of the cross deals with our emotion; when our will is especially strong, the death of the cross breaks our stubborn will. Hence, the way of a Christian depends upon the cross.

Sometimes we sense that our will is too strong and that we should suppress it so that it would not be so strong; sometimes we also feel that our emotion is too strong and that we should change it so that we would not lose our temper easily. But this does not work; this is not the way of a Christian. The way of a Christian depends on God's mercy to reveal that the death of Christ on the cross has terminated our mind, emotion, and will and that this death has entered into us and is operating in us. When our will is stubborn, the death of the cross will touch our will, and our will will be defeated. The cross is like a long sword that chops our will off at the "waist," and immediately our will succumbs. In the same way, our emotion will be softened, and our mind will be restrained. At that time, the Holy Spirit will be able to move within us in a spontaneous way.

A will that is no longer stubborn, an emotion that is no longer wild, and an unrestrained mind that no longer hinders God show that the cross has worked in our soul, and the Holy Spirit has a free way to move in us. Hence, the way of a Christian is to allow the death of Christ on the cross to have the inward ground to work.

SPIRITUAL EXPERIENCES DEPENDING ON SEEING AND NOT ON CONSECRATION

Question: In the spiritual experience of a Christian, does consecration follow immediately after baptism?

Answer: Strictly speaking, consecration has a limited impact on one's spiritual experiences. After a person believes in the Lord and is saved, he should consecrate himself, but strictly speaking, consecration alone is not enough in one's spiritual experience. Even though many people have thoroughly consecrated themselves, they still have never seen the cross. Christianity appeals to many people who have a desire to consecrate themselves in a thorough way; they are willing to give up their position and wealth in the world and to focus only on His work. There are not just a few people in this category. Nevertheless, they deviate in their spiritual experiences because they have not seen the cross.

With regard to speaking on consecration, throughout the two thousand years of church history no place can be compared with the Keswick Convention in England. These meetings are still held twice a year. People have traveled from Europe and America as if they were on a pilgrimage in order to attend the convention, and the hotel business makes much profit from this. The book *The Spirit of Christ* says that the Keswick Convention also has branch associations in India and South Africa. The focus of the convention is consecration. They think that the reason a person does not know how to take the Lord's way, does not have the presence of the Lord, and does not have light in reading the Bible is a lack of consecration. In other words, if a person wants to have the strength to take the Lord's way, the presence of the Lord, and light, he must consecrate himself. They consider consecration to be the turning point in all spiritual matters.

It is only in recent years that many people have begun to realize that consecration cannot solve the problems of a Christian and that it is not the way of a Christian. In response to this realization God raised up Mrs. Penn-Lewis to show people that the way of a Christian is not with consecration but with the cross. I am not belittling consecration, because we are consecrated ones and we have even consecrated ourselves more than once. However, consecration is not the way of a Christian; it cannot solve the problems of a Christian.

In the meetings many brothers and sisters have been touched by the Lord to kneel down and consecrate themselves to Him. This is good. But we need to ask how much we know spiritual matters after our consecration. Although our consecration causes us to be more zealous for the Lord, does it cause us to love the Lord more, to know the Lord more, or to see the death of the cross more? Consecration does not need seeing, it merely needs encouragement and exhortation. But in order for us to see the death of the cross, encouragement and exhortation are futile. Preaching the doctrine of the cross without seeing the cross is only a sermon. The listeners may be touched to shed tears and give themselves and everything to the Lord, but this kind of speaking can be compared to exhorting people to be humble and faithful; it is a word of exhortation, not a word of revelation. As long as the speaker is eloquent, this kind of word will be able to move listeners in their emotion and cause them to shed tears and bow their heads to consecrate themselves. In the end, however, the more people appreciate this kind of speaking, the more difficult it will be for them to see. The word of the cross requires our eyes to be opened to see a spiritual matter; hence, seeing is such a great matter.

CHAPTER TWELVE

QUESTIONS AND ANSWERS CONCERNING CHRIST AND THE CROSS

In this chapter we will speak concerning Christ and the cross.

THE EXPERIENCE OF ROMANS 7

Question: How does the experience portrayed in Romans 7 relate to the way of the cross?

Answer: Among those who study the Bible and pursue spirituality, there has been much controversy concerning Romans 7 during the past few centuries. In his exposition of Romans, W. H. Griffith Thomas said that Romans 7 was not the experience of Paul after his salvation. Griffith Thomas based his statement on the following points. First, Romans 7 was Paul's experience as a Jew under the law; it was his experience of the Jewish religion. This is a strong point. If chapter 7 was Paul's experience after his salvation, he would not have used the word *now* in 8:1. His saying "now then…to those who are in Christ Jesus" indicates that formerly he was not in Christ. Second, in his concluding word in Romans 7, Paul declared that he was a person corrupted in the flesh and, as such a one, cried out, "Who will deliver me from the body of this death?" (v. 24). He later found the answer; he found that he could be delivered through the Lord Jesus Christ. This shows that his experiences in chapter 7 were not in Christ.

Third, all who have studied the Bible in depth acknowledge that even though Romans 7 follows chapter 6, it does not connect the thought in chapter 6 to the thought in chapter 8. Some people say that chapter 7 is Paul's experience after his salvation, and others say that it is his experience prior to his salvation. Everyone acknowledges that chapter 7 is a big parenthesis according to its content. In other words, we can read chapter 8 immediately following chapter 6, because chapter 8 is the continuation of chapter 6. In chapter 6, when speaking of being delivered from sin, Paul intended to show that because we are not under law but under grace, we have been delivered from sin, and sin has no power over us. He then inserted a parenthesis to explain the function of the law. Hence, when speaking of those under the law, Paul says that the law lords it over a man as long as he lives (7:1). Since we have died in Christ, the law can no longer lord it over us. Even if we wanted to live under the law, this would be futile. Therefore, Paul used his past experience as an example, saying that even though he willed and strived, eventually all he had was a heart to will but not the power to do what he willed; he prostrated himself before the law. It seemed as if the law was helping him, but in reality it was doing him harm; there was nothing he could do to fulfill the law. As a result, he felt so wretched that he cried out, "Who will deliver me from the body of this death?" (v. 24).

Those who assume that Romans 7 was Paul's experience after his salvation base their consideration on Paul's use of the expression *the inner man* in verse 22: "For I delight in the law of God according to the inner man." They think that if Paul were not saved, he could not refer to *the inner man.* Since Paul was not yet regenerated as a Jew under the law, how could he have an inner man? It is true that in the New Testament *the inner man* refers to a regenerated being, but in the context of Romans 7, *the inner man* does not refer to a regenerated new man. In verse 22, Paul said that he delighted in the law of God according to the inner man; then in verse 23, he referred to the law of his mind. Moreover, in verse 25, he said, "With the mind I myself serve the law of God." The *mind* in verses 23 and 25 is rendered *heart* in the Chinese Union Version. The Greek word is *nous,* which refers to the mind, a part in the soul. We consider that we have a body outwardly, which is called the outer man, and that we have two parts inwardly, the soul and the spirit. In the soul are the mind, emotion, and will, and in the spirit are the conscience, intuition, and fellowship. The spirit is in man's innermost part, but the soul is also in man. Therefore, does *the inner man* in Romans 7 refer to the spirit or to the soul? According to the context, we know that it refers to the mind. In 7:25 Paul said that with the mind he himself served the law of God. In verse 22 he said that he delighted in the law of God according to the inner man. This shows that here the inner man refers to the mind.

We cannot say that *the inner man* in Romans 7 refers to the person in our spirit simply because 2 Corinthians 4:16 mentions the inner man. In Romans 7 the inner man refers to the soul, not to the spirit as the regenerated inner man. Paul willed to please God, but there was a different law in his members warring against the law of his mind. This is a war between reason and lust (vv. 22-23). This picture shows that even though a person may not be saved, he has outer members and an inner mind. His mind wants to do good, but the lust in his members prevents him from fulfilling his desire. Hence, the inner man in Romans 7 must refer to one's mind.

Although Romans 7 speaks of Paul's experience prior to his salvation, for many of us it is our experience after salvation.

THE EXPERIENCES OF ROMANS 7 AND GALATIANS 5

Question: How do we experience Romans 8:6: "For the mind set on the flesh is death, but the mind set on the spirit is life and peace"?

Answer: Even though Romans 7 was Paul's experience prior to his salvation, it has become the experience of many Christians after their salvation. Paul, as a Jew, strictly kept the law under the teaching of the Jews before he was saved. In Philippians 3:6 he said that as to the law, he was blameless. In contrast, we, the Gentiles, were living in dissoluteness before our salvation. After repenting and believing into the Lord Jesus, we immediately have the concept that we must no longer live dissolutely but conduct ourselves properly. This concept makes us those who live under the law, that is, it makes us "Sauls" living under the law, just as Paul was Saul when he was living under the law. We should live under the cross of Christ after our salvation. However, because of the influence of the tree of the knowledge of good and evil, we think that since we did many wrong things in the past and now have repented and believed in the Lord, we should change our conduct. This places us in the same position as Paul before his salvation, when he was Saul in Judaism.

Moreover, many of the believers at the time when Paul wrote the book of Romans were like the Christians of today; they were Judaistic believers, even though they had believed in the Lord Jesus. They did not know God's salvation; rather, according to their natural concept, they tried to do good and keep the law. This unknowingly brought them back into the Jewish religion. Before their salvation some Chinese have also had the experience of Romans 7. They paid much attention to virtue and morality and tried their best to do good, but later found out that even though they wanted to do good in their mind, there was a different law warring against them. So they wrote books that portray the same situation that Paul depicted in Romans 7. This shows that they had these experiences before they were saved and became Christians.

Some gospel friends might ask, "You say that when the Lord Jesus enters into people, He gives them a sense of right and wrong in different matters. Many of us who have never heard the gospel already know that certain matters are wrong, and we also have a sense within us. For example, we know it is not right for a couple to quarrel. How does this differ from the Lord Jesus being against the flesh of a person after their salvation?" We must see that the struggle in Romans 7 is different from the war between the Holy Spirit and the flesh in Galatians 5. The struggle in Romans 7 is not spiritual; it is a struggle between the mind with its reason and the flesh with its lust. This struggle is not a recent discovery; it has been here for a long time. It has nothing to do with the spirit.

Today, however, our experience is more complicated. After we are saved and consecrated, we have the life that is described in Galatians 5, but it is intermixed with the life that is illustrated in Romans 7. We have the experience of the

Holy Spirit warring against the flesh as well as the struggle between the law of good in our mind and the law of death in our flesh. We can have the experience of Romans 7 as well as the experience of Galatians 5. What is spoken of in Romans 7 can still be our experience. However, after experiencing the failure in Romans 7, we can enter into the glorious reality in Romans 8.

OVERCOMING THE SELF AND THE ENEMY
BY SETTING THE MIND ON THE SPIRIT

Question: In my experience I have an uncomfortable feeling when I am rebuked, but this feeling vanishes when I set my mind on the spirit. Is this an experience of Romans 7 and 8?

Answer: This experience has nothing to do with Romans 7. This chapter speaks of trying to obey the law of God with the mind but inwardly being frustrated. For example, the law says that we should not covet; thus, we do not want to covet. Consequently in the "right" circumstances covetousness will be activated in us, and we will fail in spite of all our attempts to not covet. Moreover, the more we try not to covet, the stronger our covetousness will become. This is the experience described in Romans 7. Paul said that we should not covet, for this is one of the Ten Commandments. After receiving this commandment, we may resolve to be absolute in keeping the law. However, in the "right" circumstance, we may be shaken inwardly; the more we try not to covet a particular thing, the more actively we will covet it. In the end we will realize that even though to will is present with us, we have no power; when the "right" circumstances come our way, we can do nothing. Hence, the experience in Romans 7 has nothing to do with the spirit. Man tries to obey the law of God with his mind, but he eventually fails because he is frustrated inwardly.

For example, a believer may read about honoring his parents in the Ten Commandments and in the books of Ephesians and Colossians (Eph. 6:1-3; Col. 3:20). After seeing this, he may immediately receive it in his mind and pray, "O Lord, forgive me for not honoring my parents in the past. I will honor my parents from this day forward." However, when a certain situation arises, his flesh that wants to honor his parents fails. There is a law in the flesh that cannot fulfill the commandment. The Bible also requires man to be meek and humble. After reading this, one may be touched and therefore decide to obey this word. However, when the situation changes and he tries to be meek and humble, he will fail. Instead, he is full of pride and temper. This is the experience of Romans 7.

We cannot enter Romans 8 through Romans 7; rather, chapter 8 is a continuation of chapter 6. Both chapters 6 and 8 show that we need to see that we are in Christ and in the Holy Spirit. These two "seeings" are actually one. Romans 6:3 says, "Are you ignorant that all of us who have been baptized into Christ Jesus have been baptized into His death?" To be baptized into Christ's death is to be baptized into Christ, that is, to grow together with Him in His death and resurrection (v. 5). Then chapter 8 speaks of "those who are in Christ Jesus" (v. 1). Hence, we see that chapter 8 is a continuation of chapter 6 and that chapter 7 is only a parenthetical word.

First, we need to see that we are in Christ Jesus. However, chapter 7 can become our experience because we are not clear concerning this status. Romans 6:3 asks emphatically, "Are you ignorant…," indicating that even though we should know this, we do not know it and are not clear about it. Since we have been saved and baptized into Christ Jesus, we should know that we are in Christ, yet we are not clear about this. Therefore, the first item of our experience in chapter 8 is related to our eyes being opened to see that we are in Christ Jesus.

Second, we need to see that as those who are in Christ Jesus, we have been baptized into Christ; we have been baptized into His death and buried with Him. We have also been raised with Him. It is not a matter of doing good or evil; as long as our old man has been terminated through death and burial with Him, we will be raised with Him. Then we will experience the liberating work of the Holy Spirit, the Spirit of life, who is in us. In brief, we need to see that we are in Christ, we need to see that we are in Christ's death and resurrection, and we need to see that the Holy Spirit, the life-giving Spirit, the law of the Spirit of life, is in us.

After seeing these three items, we need to cooperate with Him. The law of the Spirit of life in us requires our cooperation, by setting our mind on the Spirit of life (8:5-6). Our mind occupies a major part of our soul, and our soul is our personality, our representative. In our flesh there is the law of sin, the satanic life; in our spirit there is the divine life. As far as our fallen flesh is concerned, we belong to Satan; however, the divine life is in our regenerated spirit. In other words, even though Satan is in our flesh, God has come into our spirit. Both God and Satan are in us.

Before the fall of Adam, man was outside the realm of good and evil. However, when Adam fell and ate of the tree of the knowledge of good and evil, the satanic life entered into man's flesh, becoming the law of sin and of death in man's flesh. At our salvation, we exercised our spirit to receive the Lord who is the Spirit; He entered into us, and we now have the divine life with the law of the Spirit of life in our spirit. Hence, there are two laws within us: one is the law of sin and of death, which is the issue of Satan entering into our flesh, and the other is the law of the Spirit of life, which is the issue of God entering into our spirit. Whether we follow Satan by standing with our flesh or follow God by standing with our spirit, it all depends on us. Our personality is represented by our soul, and a major part of our soul is our mind. Hence, our mind plays a crucial role. If we set our mind on the flesh, we will stand with the flesh and follow Satan; however, if we set our mind on the spirit, we will stand with the spirit and follow God. The mind set on the spirit is life and peace (v. 6).

We are situated between God's enemy, Satan, and God. The strength of the enemy is in our flesh, but the power of God is in our spirit. The side that we lean on depends on where we choose to set our mind. If we choose the spirit, the pneumatic Christ will immediately gain ground in us. When Christ comes, the cross will come, and the issue will be verse 13, which says, "If by the Spirit you put to death the practices of the body, you will live." If we stand with the spirit, we will defeat the enemy by the cross.

We must not confuse Romans 7 and 8. In Romans 7, man is a captive who wills to break away from the usurpation of the flesh. However, every time he struggles, he is attacked and defeated; therefore, he must dutifully surrender to the flesh, to Satan. This can be compared to a mouse that has been cornered by a cat. As soon as the mouse moves, the cat pounces on the mouse and throws it up in the air. In the experience of Romans 7, when a man struggles, trying not to covet or not to have filthy thoughts, the "cat" immediately pounces on him. The law of sin comes to subdue man as soon as he makes up his mind to do good; man has no way to overcome. Instead, man needs deliverance, the deliverance that is in Christ.

After this painful experience Paul said, "Who will deliver me from the body of this death? Thanks be to God, through Jesus Christ our Lord!" (7:24-25). We are unable to overcome, but the Lord comes to be our deliverance. In 8:1 Paul said, "There is now then no condemnation to those who are in Christ Jesus." Although the Deliverer has come, we must still ask ourselves: On whose side are we? Are we on the enemy's side or on Christ's side? Are we on the side of the flesh or on the side of the Spirit? In our experience we do not enter into the experience of chapter 8 because we have had sufficient failures in chapter 7. Rather, we enter into the experience of Romans 8 because our eyes have been opened. When we give ourselves to the Spirit, rely on the Spirit, choose the Spirit, and stand with the Spirit, we put to death the enemy in the flesh by the Spirit and thereby overcome him.

ENTERING INTO THE EXPERIENCE
OF ROMANS 8 BY SEEING

Question: In my experience it takes me a long time to set my mind on the spirit. How should I experience this matter?

Answer: At Paul's conversion, the light of the universe came to him and terminated everything in him. Moreover, because the law of the Spirit of life indwelt him, in every circumstance he endeavored to set his mind on the spirit, not the flesh. However, this is not our experience. After we were saved, we may not have seen much of the cross. After attending meetings for a period of time, we receive help and our inner being is unveiled a little more. This makes it easier for us to set our mind on the spirit, but it depends entirely on how much light we have received. The more we see, the more we are able to set our mind on the spirit. Eventually, without consciously setting our mind on the spirit, our mind is already set on the spirit.

The light that Paul saw was great. He saw that the entire old creation was terminated on the cross, that Christ had become everything in him, and that He, as the Holy Spirit, had dealt with all things in him. Hence, in Paul's living and service to God, there was no ground for the flesh. In our experience, however, because of our inadequate seeing of the flesh, the Holy Spirit, the cross, and Christ in our daily living, we may be inwardly troubled, and it is difficult for us to set our mind on the spirit. As we receive more dealings and have more experiences inwardly, however, it will become easier to set our mind on the spirit. The more we exercise, the easier it will be for us to set our mind on the spirit, and the more we will know that we need to stand with the Holy Spirit. Thus, in our experience everything depends on the seeing of light. Nothing is more crucial than receiving light.

Please bear in mind that we are ushered into the experience of Romans 8 through seeing. If someone testifies that he has the experience of chapter 8 because of the help he received in chapter 7, we cannot completely discount this, but the fact is that chapter 7 cannot usher us into the experience of chapter 8 directly. Our struggles and failures enable us to see that the flesh is incapable of pleasing God by doing good, that the flesh is unable to fulfill the will of God, and that nothing good dwells in the flesh. This causes us to be subdued and have no hope in the flesh. Hence, if we want to enter into Romans 8, we must see two aspects. First, on the positive side, we must see that we are in Christ, that we grow together with Christ in His death and resurrection, and that we are in God's life. Second, on the negative side, we must see that the flesh is not only unable to please God, it is God's enemy. If we see these two aspects clearly, we will not set our mind on the flesh in an effort to do good. We will bow our head and tell the Lord, "Lord, we give ourselves to You!"

THE REALM OF THE FLESH
BEING THE ENTIRE OLD CREATION

Question: What is the definition of the realm of the flesh?

Answer: The ultimate definition of the realm of the flesh is the entire old creation. Before the fall, man had only the created body but not the satanic life. At the fall, the satanic life entered into man's body and changed man's body into flesh. *Body* and *flesh* are two different words in English and in Greek. Man's body was created by God with clay before the fall. However, when the satanic life entered into man, it transmuted man's body into the flesh. Therefore, the flesh denotes man's fallen body. Not only so, after the fall, man's mind replaced the spirit's leading function and subdued the soul so that the soul also followed the flesh. God called man *flesh* (Gen. 6:3) and ordained death to be man's final destiny. However, because of the Lord's mercy, we have seen that we are in Christ, that we have died and have been raised with Him, and that the Spirit of life dwells in us. Therefore, we must stand on His side and give ourselves to Him. This is what we should and must do.

THE RECEIVING AND THE PROPER APPLICATION
OF THE OUTPOURING OF THE HOLY SPIRIT

Question: What is the relationship between the experience of the cross and the outpouring of the Holy Spirit?

Answer: Before the death and resurrection of the Lord Jesus, the Holy Spirit had not yet been poured out, and the disciples had not yet received the outpouring of the Holy Spirit. In our experience, if we live by our flesh, it is unlikely that we will receive the outpouring of the Spirit of God. Even if the Holy Spirit descended upon us, if we are living by our flesh, we would apply this power in an improper way. In the Bible the first group of people to receive the outpouring of the Holy Spirit knew Christ's death and resurrection, and they allowed the Holy Spirit to dwell in them. Formerly they were in the flesh, arguing with one another concerning who was greater, with no comprehension of the spiritual things the Lord was speaking to them. In Acts 1, however, they experienced a drastic change while praying. They no longer argued with one another regarding who was greater; rather, they were able to expound the Word that they previously could not comprehend.

The fishermen of Galilee left their hometown, relatives, and occupation and followed Jesus the Nazarene with no reservation. They did not fear man's persecution and killing. This shows that this was not from themselves but from their knowledge of Christ's resurrection. In the Lord's resurrection they received the Holy Spirit and were able to live before the Lord by the Holy Spirit in them. They no longer argued in the flesh as before, and they did not want the world. They are typical examples of those who were used by the Lord. On the day of Pentecost, when the Holy Spirit descended on this group of people, they were able to be used by the Holy Spirit and could work by the power of the Holy Spirit. They had a realization of life and the inward ruling of the Holy Spirit so that when the outward power of the Holy Spirit was poured upon them, they could use it properly.

Within the past hundred years of church history, with the rise of the Pentecostal movement, many people who received the outpouring of the Holy Spirit have created many problems. They think that receiving the outpouring of the Holy Spirit is the same as receiving the Holy Spirit inwardly, that is, to receive the inner life. They do not know that the regeneration of the Holy Spirit is different from the outpouring of the Holy Spirit. In Acts 1, those who received the outpouring of the Holy Spirit were those who were praying in the upper room in Jerusalem. They were a group of people who knew resurrection. Since they were in resurrection, the contentions of their flesh were gone. Only such ones are qualified to receive the outpouring of the Holy Spirit and can properly use the Holy Spirit who is outpoured upon them. Some people, however, have not been prepared in this way. Hence, when the Holy Spirit is poured out upon them, they are puffed up because they have received the gift of the Holy Spirit.

Furthermore, some people have the erroneous concept that they should feel elated after receiving the outpouring of the Holy Spirit. For this reason, they repeatedly ask for the outpouring of the Holy Spirit for their personal enjoyment.

However, the outpouring of the Holy Spirit is not for one's personal enjoyment; it is so that the gospel may be preached to the uttermost part of the earth. When someone who is prepared and whose heart is pure receives the outpouring of the Holy Spirit, what he manifests will be normal; however, when someone with an impure motive receives the outpouring of the Holy Spirit, what he manifests will be abnormal.

Through the outpouring of the Holy Spirit, God wants to expose our genuine, inward condition. As a rule, if we desire to receive the outpouring of the Holy Spirit, we must have the experience of the cross. Without the experience of the cross, we can never use the outpouring of the Holy Spirit in a proper way. If we have our own preference and pride, we will use the outpouring of the Holy Spirit to do all kinds of strange things. Hence, whoever receives the outpouring of the Holy Spirit must receive and apply it in a proper way; this requires the experience of the cross. Without the experience of the cross, there will not be a proper response to the outpouring of the Holy Spirit.

During 1943 and 1944, there were some in the church in Tsinan, Shantung Province, who claimed that they had received the outpouring of the Holy Spirit. One of the brothers walked on the floor with all four limbs, saying that he was the colt on which the Lord Jesus rode on the way to Jerusalem. Everyone watched him with godly fear. After running intensely, this brother laid down to rest. In this way, the church in Tsinan was brought into a chaotic situation. This shows that the experience of the cross was absent; they might have received the outpouring of the Holy Spirit, but their flesh had not yet been dealt with. We can declare before the Lord that we do not oppose the outpouring of the Holy Spirit. But in order for us to receive and use the outpouring of the Holy Spirit properly, we must pass through the cross; otherwise, it will eventually cause problems.

We must remember that the outpouring of the Holy Spirit transpired after Golgotha, Christ's resurrection and ascension, and His entering into man to be man's life through the Holy Spirit. Therefore, we must know Golgotha and Christ's resurrection and ascension, we must learn to allow the flesh to pass through the dealings of the cross, be delivered from the earth and earthly attractions, and allow the life in ascension to solve all of our problems. Then it will be easy to receive the outpouring of the Holy Spirit and to apply it profitably.

RECEIVING THE OUTPOURING OF THE HOLY SPIRIT BASED UPON THE EXPERIENCE OF THE CROSS

Question: Does a person still need the outpouring of the Holy Spirit after experiencing the cross?

Answer: After experiencing the cross, we still need the outpouring of the Holy Spirit. However, when we have an adequate amount of experience of the cross, we will no longer need to plead for the outpouring of the Holy Spirit. This does not mean that the outpouring, the outward filling, of the Holy Spirit is unrelated to our praying in spirit; the two are closely related. If we experience the cross and pray more in spirit, we will not need to pray for the outpouring of the Holy Spirit, but the Holy Spirit will certainly be poured out. We will not need to pray for the outward filling of the Holy Spirit, but we will have the outward filling of the Holy Spirit. We will not wait for the feeling that the Spirit has been outpoured before we preach the gospel. Rather, we will speak by the Spirit and others will spontaneously sense power coming out from us. We must have the experience of the cross and then receive the outpouring of the Holy Spirit based on this experience.

THE ULTIMATE PURPOSE OF THE CROSS BEING THE FULFILLMENT OF GOD'S WILL

Question: How does the experience of the cross relate to the dividing of the soul and the spirit? What is the experience of the cross? Is it the all-inclusive death of Christ that becomes the experience of the cross in us?

Answer: When we see what it means to be in Christ, to die and be raised with Christ, and to have the move of the Holy Spirit in us, we will know what it is to be under the Holy Spirit. If we see this, we will know clearly what is of ourselves and what is of the spirit. Here the spirit does not refer to the Holy Spirit but to our human spirit. Our spirit is connected to our soul. Only when we are under the cross will we be able to discern what is of the spirit and what is of the soul.

When the Lord Jesus was on the earth, He always stood on the position of denying the self. For example, His brothers in the flesh said to Him, "Depart from here and go into Judea, so that Your disciples also may behold Your works which You are doing; for no one does anything in secret and himself seeks to be known openly. If You do these things, manifest Yourself to the world" (John 7:3-4). His brothers in the flesh thought that He should go and keep the feast in Jerusalem, instead of hiding Himself, so as to manifest Himself to the world. But the Lord Jesus said, "My time has not yet come, but your time is always ready...I am not going up to this feast, because My time has not yet been fulfilled" (vv. 6, 8). When He was on earth, He completely put Himself to death. This was to bear the cross. Eventually, He was crucified. Before His crucifixion, He told the Father, "Not as I will, but as You will...If this cannot pass away unless I drink it, Your will be done" (Matt. 26:39, 42). Hence, the ultimate purpose of the cross in us is the will of God; it is to rid us of our self and to let God and His will be fulfilled in us.

When the Lord Jesus was on the earth, He lived in death until He went to the cross to fully accomplish death. When we are saved, Christ enters into us with the demand of death, requiring us to be freed from the self through His death. If we receive the demand of His death, we will receive the cross, that is, we will experience the cross.

THE SHINING OF GOD KILLING OUR SELF

Question: What is the difference between death and the demand of death?

Answer: In experience, the demand of death is death itself. If we have not had this experience, we will think that death and the demand of death are two separate items. If we tell the Lord, "O Lord, I am willing to let You live out from me," immediately the demand of death will be upon us. Our self may be very strong, but when the demand of death comes, the strong self will be terminated. Soon after praying such a prayer, the Lord's speaking will come to show that we still have the self in certain aspects. We may immediately say, "O Lord, yes." At this time we may still rely on the self, but death continues to kill the particular aspect that the Lord has pointed out. What we experience may be only a small "surgery," a small enlightening. When Paul encountered the great light, all of his being was terminated; his flesh, natural man, and self were not able to rise up. God's shining kills our self; this is the experience of the cross, but there is a difference in degree with different people.

THE CROSS BEING FOR TERMINATION, NOT FOR SUFFERING

Question: Does the cross become heavier or deeper?

Answer: There is a hymn that says, "The cross that He gave may be heavy, / But it ne'er outweighs His grace" (*Hymns,* #722). This kind of utterance is not scriptural; we cannot find it in the Bible. In experience, however, this utterance is correct. This is like the experience Madame Guyon describes in her book *Fragrance of Myrrh.* However, we must carefully study this saying, because it has too much of the Catholic background. Catholicism understands the cross as a suffering, and this concept has spread to Christianity in China; thus, many Christians also regard the cross as a suffering.

Thomas á Kempis once said that if we remove one cross, we will receive a heavier one. How many crosses are there? There is only one cross; there are not many crosses. From the experience of the Mystics, the expression that á Kempis used is correct but not scriptural. From the perspective of the truth, there is only one cross. The Mystics had such an experience because they loved the Lord, earnestly desired the Lord, absolutely put themselves aside, and let the Lord reign in them. However, they did not receive the light that we see. They considered their wives, their superiors, and the leading ones in the church as crosses. How this differs from the light the Lord has given us! The thought that the cross becomes heavier is the result of insufficient light concerning the cross. The work of the cross can be deeper but not heavier; only suffering is heavier.

We need to be clear that suffering is not the cross. Both the Catholic Church and Christianity think that the cross is a suffering. However, even though suffering and the cross are somewhat related, suffering is not the cross. The cross is for our termination. When Christ puts the demand of the cross in us, His intention is to terminate us; He requires us to surrender to Him. When He shows us that certain aspects of our personality are too strong, the cross requires us to be broken; however, we may be unwilling to submit. Then He must use an outward environment of suffering to intensify the light of the cross in us, to the extent that we will surrender and completely yield to Him. Even though we should surrender and be broken, we may be unwilling; even though we know that the Lord has an inward demand, we may be unwilling to obey. At such times the Lord will raise up the environment to deal with us, to compel us, and to defeat us. This is the reason Catholics say that the cross is a suffering. However, the cross itself is not a suffering. When we are unwilling to submit to the demand of the cross, God uses the outward environment as a means to help us. God uses the light of the cross inwardly and the dealing of the environment outwardly to subdue us. In brief, the cross is the inward light; the suffering is the outward environment.

THE DEATH OF THE CROSS BEING PAINFUL YET SWEET

Question: It seems that those who experience the cross suffer a great deal. Does the Lord's cup of suffering refer to the suffering of the cross?

Answer: Those who are unwilling to be subdued in their experience of the cross will feel pain. We may see the light, love the Lord, and know that we need to cooperate with the Lord, and still be unwilling to immediately submit and be subdued, because of our opinion. If this is our situation, the environment gradually grinds away this particular resistance in our being so that we will be subdued, regardless of our preference. The breaking work of the cross in us is in coordination with the outward environment. However, if we are willing to submit to the cross, we will not need the many outward circumstances and difficulties. The principle is that outward circumstances and sufferings cooperate with the light of the cross within us in order to subdue, break, and defeat us.

Although the cross is for termination, no one should say that there is no pain in relation to the cross. It is true that suffering is involved with the cross, but the focus is not on suffering but on death and termination. The Lord Jesus was willing to take the cup of suffering. But His focus was not on suffering but on the cup. As far as the cup is concerned, it is sweet. Experience tells us that when we receive the death of the cross, it is painful yet exceedingly sweet.

THE HOLY SPIRIT BEING
UPON THE DISCIPLES OUTWARDLY
BEFORE THE RESURRECTION OF THE LORD

Question: The Lord Jesus was with His disciples before His crucifixion. At that time, did the disciples have the Spirit of the Lord in them?

Answer: Before the crucifixion of the Lord Jesus, based on the fact that He had not yet resurrected and ascended to heaven, the disciples did not yet have the Spirit of the Lord. However, the disciples, like the Old Testament saints, had the work of the Holy Spirit upon them; they did not have the Holy Spirit entering and indwelling them. It was only after the Lord's death, resurrection, and ascension that He breathed Himself into the disciples in resurrection, and the Holy Spirit began to indwell them (John 20:22). Although they did not have the Holy Spirit indwelling them prior to this, they had the Holy Spirit upon them as in the Old Testament.

THE PUTTING TO DEATH OF THE CROSS
BEING THE SAME AS THE KILLING OF THE CROSS

Question: After seeing the great light of the cross and the putting to death of our flesh, if we sense that our death is a suffering, have we truly died? If we are dead, will we be like Paul and never sense that it is a suffering?

Answer: If we have truly seen the great light of the cross, the cross will not merely be a suffering to us, even though from the human perspective, it is still a suffering. Sister M. E. Barber wrote a hymn that says, "Let the spirit praise Thee, / Though the heart be riven" (*Hymns*, #377). We often reverse the emphasis and say, "The heart is riven, though the spirit praises Thee." We should realize that the purpose of the experience of the cross is death and termination, not suffering, even though some suffering is involved in the process. Our experience confirms this.

Some people think that there is a contradiction in the Bible because it speaks, on the one hand, of our crucifixion through the cross of Christ and, on the other hand, of the putting to death by the Holy Spirit. In our experience the putting to death of the self is based on seeing our "co-crucifixion" with Christ. Only those who have seen their co-crucifixion with Christ can experience the killing of the cross. In 2 Corinthians 4:10, the "putting to death," the killing, the deadening, is the operation of the death of the cross which kills us daily. This daily killing is the putting to death in Romans 8:13 and Colossians 3:5. Putting to death is based upon the effect of the killing of the cross. Hence, the putting to death, the killing, and death are all the same thing.

ABOUT THE AUTHOR

Witness Lee was born in 1905 in northern China and raised in a Christian family. At age 19 he was fully captured for Christ and immediately consecrated himself to preach the gospel for the rest of his life. Early in his service, he met Watchman Nee, a renowned preacher, teacher, and writer. Witness Lee labored together with Watchman Nee under his direction. In 1934 Watchman Nee entrusted Witness Lee with the responsibility for his publication operation, called the Shanghai Gospel Bookroom.

Prior to the Communist takeover in 1949, Witness Lee was sent by Watchman Nee and his other co-workers to Taiwan to ensure that the things delivered to them by the Lord would not be lost. Watchman Nee instructed Witness Lee to continue the former's publishing operation abroad as the Taiwan Gospel Bookroom, which has been publicly recognized as the publisher of Watchman Nee's works outside China. Witness Lee's work in Taiwan manifested the Lord's abundant blessing. From a mere 350 believers, newly fled from the mainland, the churches in Taiwan grew to 20,000 in five years.

In 1962 Witness Lee felt led of the Lord to come to the United States, settling in California. During his 35 years of service in the U.S., he ministered in weekly meetings and weekend conferences, delivering several thousand spoken messages. Much of his speaking has since been published as over 400 titles. Many of these have been translated into over fourteen languages. He gave his last public conference in February 1997 at the age of 91.

He leaves behind a prolific presentation of the truth in the Bible. His major work, *Life-study of the Bible,* comprises over 25,000 pages of commentary on every book of the Bible from the perspective of the believers' enjoyment and experience of God's divine life in Christ through the Holy Spirit. Witness Lee was the chief editor of a new translation of the New Testament into Chinese called the Recovery Version and directed the translation of the same into English. The Recovery Version also appears in a number of other languages. He provided an extensive body of footnotes, outlines, and spiritual cross references. A radio broadcast of his messages can be heard on Christian radio stations in the United States. In 1965 Witness Lee founded Living Stream Ministry, a non-profit corporation, located in Anaheim, California, which officially presents his and Watchman Nee's ministry.

Witness Lee's ministry emphasizes the experience of Christ as life and the practical oneness of the believers as the Body of Christ. Stressing the importance of attending to both these matters, he led the churches under his care to grow in Christian life and function. He was unbending in his conviction that God's goal is not narrow sectarianism but the Body of Christ. In time, believers began to meet simply as the church in their localities in response to this conviction. In recent years a number of new churches have been raised up in Russia and in many eastern European countries.

OTHER BOOKS PUBLISHED BY
Living Stream Ministry

Titles by Witness Lee:

Titles by Watchman Nee:

Available at
Christian bookstores, or contact Living Stream Ministry
2431 W. La Palma Ave. • Anaheim, CA 92801
1-800-549-5164 • www.livingstream.com